WHAT HAPPENS when a professional illustrator gets an assignment? When they hang up the phone after speaking with an art director, what do they do? After they finish reading the text and specs off a fax, what next? Do they rush to their drawing boards and dash off two dozen sketches? Or do they fold up into a lotus position and chant? Where do their ideas come from? How important is research? How do ideas become graphic representations of those ideas? How many stages of approval by the client are required? What are some tricks to keep changes to a minimum? How long does the whole process take? How do they keep excited and challenged about making pictures?

The Pro-Illustration series explores these and other questions and provides answers. In each volume, nine top professionals demonstrate how they proceed from initial assignment to final illustration. In easy to understand steps, they'll share with you their thought processes and techniques.

By exploring a variety of methods, emerging illustrators will find the most effective way to communicate ideas. In the Pro-Illustration series many techniques will be demonstrated, so if cutting tiny pieces of frisket and wielding an airbrush—as Guy Billout does—is too exacting and methodical for some, perhaps painting with your hands—as Marshall Arisman does—would better suit your personality. Or consider Wilson McLean's section and you may find that you love painting in luscious oils.

You will discover that, for an illustration to be successful, it is necessary to have a concept that is equal to the execution. Beautiful technique is not enough; the point must be made with a clear visual image that can be quickly read. Yet, the concept can't outweigh the technique—the aim is for a nice marriage. It is a silent media—communication must be accomplished without words.

The world of illustration is as varied and inventive as each artist who inhabits it. As this series demonstrates, it's a world which asks only that you keep your eyes and minds open to possibility.

ILLUSTRATION, A FINE ART The sculptor David Smith defined commercial art as "Art that meets the minds and needs of other people," and fine art as "Art that meets the mind and needs of the artist." Illustrator and career-long educator Marshall Arisman suggests that illustration can function as "one outlet for work done to meet both the artists' needs and the public's. Discoveries made in painting," he says, "can be translated into illustration using the printed page as an entry to explore the possibility of word and image." Alan E. Cober, another of America's premier illustrators and teachers, puts it this way: "I am an artist. I have chosen the magazine as my vehicle for making pictures." He claims never to have enjoyed the gallery wall as much as the printed page and that his work has been seen by millions of people as a result of his pleasure in working for the print medium. Joan Hall feels that "illustration is becoming more and more creative and less dictated to by fashion than fine art itself."

MEDIA IS THE MESSAGE If you look over the description of the media used by illustrators in only one of the thirty-eight volumes of the Society of Illustrators Annual of American Illustration, you can see an extraordinary array of possibilities open to you. Traditional methods continue to predominate: oil on canvas, watercolor, and acrylic. But we see with greater frequency entries such as "Iris printouts from Illustrator 5.5 for the Macintosh computer." Artists draw using pencil, charcoal, pen and ink, pastel, crayon, and colored pencils. They make their marks on linen canvas, cotton duck, masonite, wood, vinyl, all manner of illustration board with rough or smooth finishes, and on every variety of paper from Arches watercolor blocks to Japanese rice paper. They carve or scratch out their lines in etchings, linocuts, drypoint, block prints and scratchboard. They make lithographs, monotypes, or monoprints.

Those who mix their media combine any number of techniques. The collage artists and three-dimensional illustrators use any material that serves their intellectual and aesthetic needs, from centuries-old ephemera to live doves. In the Pro-Illustration series, we will show you the hows and whys of these techniques.

As in all areas of modern life, the computer is moving into illustration. Some of the illustrators in this book—like Barbara Nessim—actively use it, others are in the process

a guide to

professional techniques

by jill bossert

sponsored by

the society of illustrators

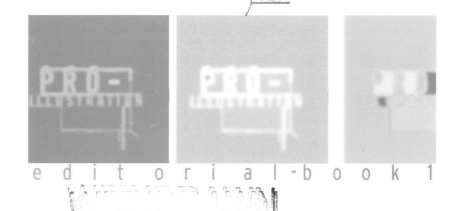

editorial-book 1

Roto Vision SA
7 rue du Bugnon
1299 Crans
Switzerland

ISBN 0-8230-6549-9

Distributors to the trade in the United States
Watson-Guptill Publications
1515 Broadway, New York, NY 10036

Published for the Society of Illustrators
128 East 63rd Street, New York, NY 10021

Distributed throughout
the rest of the world by:
Rotovision Sales Office
Sheridan House
112-116A Western Road
Hove BN3 1DD, England
Tel: +44 1273 727268
Fax: +44 1273 727269

by Jill Bossert
Designed by Stephen Byram and Eric Baker
Eric Baker Design Associates Inc.
Design Assistant; Loreena Persaud
Cover illustration by Stephen Byram
Printed in Singapore

Photography:
© 1996 by Marianne Barcellona for demonstration photographs and portraits of Marshall
Arisman, Guy Billout, Alan E. Cober, Joan Hall,
Barbara Nessim, Tim O'Brien, Mel Odom

© 1996 John Duillo for demonstration
photographs and portrait of Elaine Duillo

© 1996 Rosemary Howard for demonstration
photographs and portrait of Wilson McLean

of learning how, such as Joan Hall who sees it as a tool for collage artists, though it lacks a sensuality she likes. Guy Billout looks forward to learning to work on the computer. It will enable him to duplicate meticulous airbrush work, and because he uses photographs for reference, it will allow him to manipulate images more easily. And, he delights in the fact he won't have to wear a protective mask all day! Others won't switch— Mel Odom says he wishes he could be a wiz video artist, but he wonders what happens when the electricity fails? He now uses paint and vellum, the same materials as monks used to illuminate manuscripts in medieval times, so no one can "pull the plug." Elaine Duillo knows it's the future but fears the loss of quality; Wilson McLean won't discuss it.

Naturally, the computer, as a tool, is only as good and stimulating as the artist using it. If you are only interested in technique, flashy technical images will be all you'll get—if you have something to say, the computer is another medium of expression. Throughout the series we will show how the computer can be used creatively to make compelling images for reproduction.

Arisman counsels the following, which holds true for all forms of media: "Make pictures you know something about in which you have a personal interest. Consider the issue seriously and if you are sincere and honest with yourself, you will realize that you have something to say with your work beyond its style."

CREATIVITY Although the primary function of this book—and of the entire series—is to clearly and concisely describe the technical feats of famous illustrators, there is an aspect about making a piece of art that should be touched upon. For want of a better term, we'll call it creativity. We've tried to allude to it between the descriptions of what type of brush to use, or how to cut a perfect frisket, or what mixture of paint will produce a luminous flower petal. It cannot be taught, exactly, but it can be stimulated, and it can be allowed to, and in fact, it must be allowed to rise from within and be brought to bear upon the technical aspects of picture making. Each artist must discover it for himself or herself, as it is deeply personal and different for everyone.

As the nine artists describe the process of creating their work, invariably a moment comes when each one can no longer express that process in concrete terms. By whatever route they take to reach a satisfactory solution, and however clear the mechanics of reaching it are, there always remains a moment of mystery. Alan E. Cober simply says, "I don't know what I'm doing," which may, on the face of his accomplishments, appear disingenuous. Yet— there is a mysterious space that resides somewhere between the place where conscious problem-solving occurs and the technical knowledge and experience that is the execution. It is a place that no one can properly describe. It is a place where transcendent emotion, intellect, and graphic representation come together to create imagery that effectively touches others.

It is the home of creativity. And those who have been living creative lives for years know as little about it as those who have just begun to explore that mysterious territory. Time and experience does not obliterate it. Each assignment asks the artist to go there. A first-year student who creates a successful image—even under the burden of unformed skills—can share the sensation of the award-winning illustrator. By the same token, a thirty-year veteran must be able to experience the mystery, or the work will reflect a lack of spontaneity. Technique and old solutions will replace ingenuity and creativity.

Mel Odom likes a visual that's open to interpretation by the viewer and even by himself— a subconscious thought that he was not privy to during the act of drawing. Guy Billout says he's not sure of the true meaning of the concept as he's creating it—it's an interpretation that comes later. "There is no process," Cober says of his means at arriving at his deeply personal imagery. "I don't know where I get my ideas, they're just the things that are around." Barbara Nessim says, "Releasing my creative potential is about relaxing my conscious thought process, paying attention to my peripheral vision, and taking action (especially when I am not sure of what I am doing). Taking action is the most important part of this equation. My muse is always with me. I must trust my muse. It is my pathfinder and letting it find `me' is the fun part. Curiosity is at the heart of all my creativity." This idea is shared by many of the artists; you must allow yourself to be open to accidents. The general consensus, too, is that a certain amount of playfulness is crucial to the process. Good advice might be to indulge yourself in the things that fascinate you—the themes and meanings will take care of themselves. If you are unable to explain hard reasoning for certain choices you make, don't be alarmed— you could be right where you want to be.

Jill Bossert

There's a narrow building with a red door on 63rd Street just off Lexington Avenue in New York City. Step in when you're in the neighborhood. Better yet, journey there. Come by hook or crook or by jet or jitney. Peruse the names on the bronze plaque, then try to suppress a low whistle and the word WOW!

HALL OF FAME LAUREATES 1958-1996

Norman Rockwell 1958
Dean Cornwell 1959
Harold Von Schmidt 1959
Fred Cooper 1960
Floyd Davis 1961
Edward Wilson 1962
Walter Biggs 1963
Arthur William Brown 1964
Al Parker 1965
Al Dorne 1966
Robert Fawcett 1967
Peter Helck 1968
Austin Briggs 1969
Rube Goldberg 1970
Stevan Dohanos 1971
Ray Prohaska 1972
Jon Whitcomb 1973
Tom Lovell 1974
Charles Dana Gibson 1974
N.C. Wyeth 1974
Bernie Fuchs 1975
Maxfield Parrish 1975
Howard Pyle 1975
John Falter 1976
Winslow Homer 1976
Harvey Dunn 1976
Robert Peak 1977
Wallace Morgan 1977
J.C. Leyendecker 1977
Coby Whitmore 1978

Norman Price 1978
Frederic Remington 1978
Ben Stahl 1979
Edwin Austin Abbey 1979
Lorraine Fox 1979
Saul Tepper 1980
Howard Chandler Christy 1980
James Montgomery Flagg 1980
Stan Galli 1981
Frederic R. Gruger 1981
John Gannam 1981
John Clymer 1982
Henry P. Raleigh 1982
Eric (Carl Erickson) 1982
Mark English 1983
Noel Sickles 1983
Franklin Booth 1983
Neysa Moran McMein 1984
John LaGatta 1984
James Williamson 1984
Charles Marion Russell 1985
Arthur Burdett Frost 1985
Robert Weaver 1985
Rockwell Kent 1986
Al Hirschfeld 1986
Haddon Sundblom 1987
Maurice Sendak 1987
René Bouché 1988
Pruett Carter 1988

Robert T. McCall 1988
Erté 1989
John Held Jr. 1989
Arthur Ignatius Keller 1989
Burt Silverman 1990
Robert Riggs 1990
Morton Roberts 1990
Donald Teague 1991
Jessie Willcox Smith 1991
William A. Smith 1991
Joe Bowler 1992
Edwin A. Georgi 1992
Dorothy Hood 1992
Robert McGinnis 1993
Thomas Nast 1993
Coles Phillips 1993
Harry Anderson 1994
Elizabeth Shippen Green 1994
Ben Shahn 1994
James Avati 1995
McClelland Barclay 1995
Joseph Clement Coll 1995
Frank E. Schoonover 1995
Herb Tauss 1996
Anton Otto Fischer 1996
Winsor McCay 1996
Violet Oakley 1996
Mead Schaeffer 1996

These are the names of the artists chosen by their peers for the Society of Illustrators Hall of Fame.
Read the names again and visualize the work that has issued from those varied hands and minds. You're apt to be jolted by sheer force of the accumulative talent those names represent; and jolted still further if you ruminate on the zillions of readers who were enticed into the text of the myriad stories, books and articles, each peopled and composed into imagined places and predicaments. And think too, of the effect on the fashions and mores of their times inspired by their magazine and advertising works.
In an earlier day, swipe-happy Hollywood kept a keen eye on their output and borrowed liberally from it.
In past years the Society was Home Sweet Home for many members. That's where they hung out before the migration to the suburbs. It was the social center for the profession; the Gallery, the Bar, and the Pool Table were where the members gathered after they quit their drawing boards and easels for the day.

That custom no longer obtains. Luncheon is the big gathering time now. The pool table has long since vanished to make space for the avalanche of entries for upcoming Annual Exhibitions which have become a high point of New York's graphic scene.
The building now continually hangs exhibitions on three floors. Selections from the Permanent Collection are on view in the buzzing dining room at all times. These walls reflect the unimagined visual changes that have evolved since the early days of mostly oil, wash and charcoal works. To be sure, those mediums are still widely used, but in vastly different ways as the eyes and hands behind them reflect their times.

That means an exposure to the wizard's mix of today's hi-tech explosion of visual wonders.
The old days of illustrated fiction, as we nostalgically recall it, has disappeared down Memory Lane. But to replace it we have marvelous paperback book cover illustrators, jacket designers, skilled imaginers who depict the never-never land of Science Fiction, incredible renderers with surrealistic leanings, ingenious decorative artists, artists who think funny and draw funny, too, and a slew of creators who palm a plastic mouse around a magic pad to amazing effect.
The ghosts of Charles Dana Gibson, N.C. Wyeth, and Harvey Dunn, et. al., must spin in a smocked whirlwind at the sight of today's state of things. But, cool it Old Gents, your legacy still lingers. The human figure, though rendered now in endless new inventive ways, still prevails in the narrow building where you set the standards long ago.

Howard Munce
Honorary President, Society of Illustrators

Welcome to the Society of Illustrators, a not-for-profit educational organization founded in 1901. The mission of this Society is to promote the art of illustration. The key to the fulfillment of that mission is education. This book is a significant addition to the educational process of artists, as it is the only one created by that unique visual creator, the ILLUSTRATOR.

Art education is an ongoing process. Just look at the processes and influence displayed herein. These artists have continually sought out the works of their peers, as well as the works of the greats of the past, and added them to their own artistic stew. Among the many venues for investigation is the Society of Illustrators. Annually, over 3,000 original works are displayed in the Society of Illustrators Museum of American Illustration in group, theme, and solo shows. The Lecture Series brings to the public the presentations of as many as ten artists in one-on-one sessions and in panel discussions. Publications of contemporary and historic illustration bring to a wide international audience the top practitioners from Hall of Famers to college-level students. Videos, slides, traveling exhibitions, and membership are other avenues that are used to spread the word.

One of the leading award-winning illustrators working today is Gary Kelley. Upon receiving a Gold Medal in the Society's Annual Exhibition, he told a story which illustrates the ongoing process of art education. Gary's studio is in Cedar Falls, Iowa, a small college town surrounded by corn fields. A job he was working on was not going well. It was time, he realized, to freshen his point of view by going "out on the road." He called an illustrator friend from Ohio. They met in Chicago to see an exhibition, on its last day, of an 18th century Spanish painter. Gary returned to Cedar Falls, fully recharged, and turned out the Gold Medal winner. That's the muse that drives the pro.

Beyond the live action of exhibitions and lectures, lies the vast study hall of the printed page. Like this publication, books on theory and creative evolution, as well as commercial and fine art reference, serve to fire one's passions when needed. Would Gary Kelley have ascended to Gold without the stimulation of that Spanish painter? Maybe, but had that exhibit in Chicago been closed, his piece might have lacked a certain, special texture.

Surely, you would enjoy having these nine artists sit down in your studio and show you how they work. Given that impracticality, their efforts will serve you as presented here. In fact, their ideas and pictures can occupy an imposing place above your board or PC. Always there to break the funk or power up weak batteries.

There is validity in the title of this series: Pro-Illustration. It is indeed a profession. An artist, whether student, novice, or pro, can benefit from the unique creative techniques of the illustrator. Because of an illustration's predetermined dimension and deadline, it must conform to scale and be on time. Created for the purpose of solving a visual need, an illustration must stay within the conceptual confines of its inducer. Palette, genre, and delivery mode (traditional or digital) may also be dictated by the client. Egads! What's left?

Ah, there's the rub. Given all of these fences, illustrators take up the challenge and find solutions that overcome the hurdles. They find the twist that communicates and also keeps them enthralled as artists. They find the edge that gives this particular job a dangerous quality. And they do it day in and day out, many of them for an entire career. With that fine-tuned mental gymnastic training, an illustrator is well suited to present both the technical and the intellectual processes of the craft.

This professionalism is not new to the industry. One of its first superstars was the pen-and-ink social satirist and cultural delineator, Charles Dana Gibson (1867-1944). In the pages of Life, from the 1880s to the 1920s, he depicted love, liberty, and the pursuit of happiness. At a recent exhibition at the Society of over a hundred of Gibson's originals, time and again the contemporary professional illustrators wondered: "Why did he make it so difficult? Why did he add that element which must have taken a great deal of time to work out? Why did he add that extra character, architectural element, or punch line?" The answer lies in the challenge. The simple is too easy; the difficult keeps you fresh.

Look at these nine professional solutions. Easy, you say? Read the book and issue yourself the challenge.

Terrence Brown
Director, Society of Illustrators

This is the first communication of the assignment we sent each artist: *"The Sunday magazine supplement of a major newspaper is preparing a Valentine issue. The cover story is a survey and analysis of the state of Love as the century draws to a close. A variety of topics and views will be presented, all of which need to be illustrated."*

Then we asked each illustrator to focus on a particular aspect of love: an overview, first love, historical romance, weddings, sensual love, erotic love, computer love, adultery, and divorce. An attempt was made to match the style of each artist with the subject matter. One of the greatest pleasures was to see the amazingly inventive ways each one took their theme and warmed to it. Exciting surprises abounded—all in the context of a relatively specific editorial assignment. It should be noted here that the number of steps each artist takes to fulfill an assignment does not indicate by any measure the difficulty or ease with which they accomplish their tasks. For example, Elaine Duillo spent far longer on each step than Tim O'Brien did, though he went through more individual steps. Value is not placed on the amount of work done, but what the work produces. Some techniques are fulfilling to individuals for unknown reasons. Wilson McLean is in love with paint and color and will spend weeks on a painting enriching its subtle shadings, while Barbara Nessim can spend hours in front of a computer screen making her drawings move. There is no right way. But one thing is quite clear: all these artists are perfectionists in their own way. Obsession seems to be a necessary ingredient to being a successful illustrator.

THE ASSIGNMENT: *well aware of marshall arisman's* dark style, it seemed prudent not to assign him one of the more sentimental aspects of love. He was asked to focus on the idea of adultery, which he agreed to do with little discussion. Although he was contacted before the photographic and interview sessions, **no other exchanges took place regarding the concept, and no sketches were submitted.** In view of his professionalism and idiosyncratic style, his assurance **that an illustration would be produced by the deadline was sufficient.** THE THOUGHT PROCESS: Art Directors come to Marshall Arisman, he says, for some "emotional content rather for narrative significance—they're looking for a feeling." The very open assignments require a redefinition and a narrowing down by the artist. The first step in focusing the concept is to look up the word in the dictionary and write it down. For "adultery" he wrote: "Sexual intercourse between a married man and a woman not his wife, or bet- *ween a married woman etc." he then consulted with men he knew who had had some experience with the subject. generally he found that a pattern emerged: most men were looking for a sexual fantasy, rather than a romantic one. rather than placing a man and woman together in a real place, he would make the man a reality, and then consider the idea of a woman as fantasy. he made a list of fantasies, and by free association wrote down the word "mermaid." to him it was a symbol, an icon—and he liked the ambiguity of the symbol. in his experience mermaids are depicted as cute, but because adultery is a serious situation, he felt it should not be as much a mermaid as a fish—keeping it a little spooky. in his sketches, he placed the mermaid somewhere near the head of the man, where the fantasy life originates. in his discussions about the subject, he found there is always an outside presence—either religious or simply the fear of being caught. often children are the ones "most freaked out," so he thought that he could incorporate "innocence" as*

ARISMAN'S LARGE, LIGHT-FILLED STUDIO IN MID-TOWN MANHATTAN HAS SEVERAL ROOMS DEVOTED TO WORKS ON CANVAS WHICH HE HAS CREATED FOR GALLERY EXHIBITION. A SERIES OF FIFTEEN MONKEY POR- TRAITS, ON LAVISH GOLD BACK- GROUNDS, DOMINATES ONE WALL. THEY ARE PART OF AN ALL-ENCOMPASSING PROJECT—A KIND OF IRONIC, YET SOMEHOW INVESTIGATORY ANTHROPO- LOGICAL SURVEY OF HIS FICTIVE "LAND OF SACRED MONKEYS." SCATTERED AROUND ARE MONKEY DEATH MASKS, TOTEM SCULPTURES PRESUMABLY CRE- ATED BY THE SACRED MONKEYS, AS WELL AS AN ILLUSTRATED MANUSCRIPT DETAILING THEIR LIVES. IT IS IN THIS IMAGINATIVE ATMOSPHERE, WHICH CON- TAINS HUMOR AND MYSTERY, THAT ARISMAN CREATES HIS ILLUSTRATIONS.

editorial[arisman

the observer—as symbolized by the child's drawing. it didn't literally mean the man or woman had a child, but if it was so construed, that worked as well.

arisman prefers not to show sketches to art directors. he uses his sketches as diagrams for himself—without the emotion—using them to free associate, as he does with words. these "diagrams" he would never show, but, if necessary, he would create ones that are closer to the finish. he is not asked for color sketches because most art directors are familiar with his palette and know that whatever he turns in on a sketch, will not necessarily be the colors he ends up with in the finish.

REFERENCE:

Over the years, Arisman has collected many books and scrap. He has a "stack" of things and knows everything in it, but not necessarily its location. When he becomes frustrated with the disarray, he categorizes it, but within six months it's in a messy pile once again. Normally he needs three or four pieces of reference to cover the elements of a story. "To me, illustration, unlike painting where changes can occur throughout, must be fully considered in advance. I don't even start artwork until I saturate myself with the problem. So, I go to the dictionary, the library— I do anything to get familiar enough with all aspects of the where, when, how of a problem— then I'm not so self-conscious about it."

THE STEPS:

1 Arisman "talks to himself in pictures" creating sketches using Higgens Black Magic ink and a brush.

2 For illustrations, Arisman works on paper rather than canvas for two reasons: the oil paint dries faster on paper and it's "less precious" to him. He uses a 23x29 inch, Strathmore 3-ply plate finish rag paper. Because he paints with his hands, he can't work much smaller than that— even if the reproduction is only two inches.

He pushpins each sheet onto a wall that carries evidence of many other paintings. Because untreated paper soaks up the paint too fast, he coats it with inexpensive white oil paint straight from the tube mixed with turpentine in a cup. Applied with an old paint brush, it gives the surface a little texture. Unlike gesso, oil paint does not buckle the paper. He prepares twenty sheets at a time, allowing two or three days' drying time. The paper is not of archival quality, so the illustrations are not necessarily permanent.

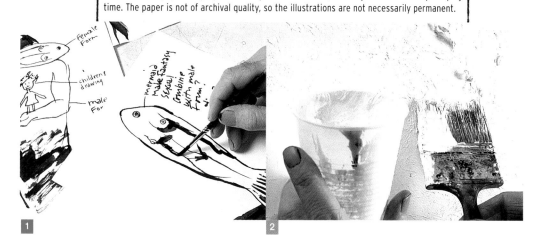

1   2

3

4

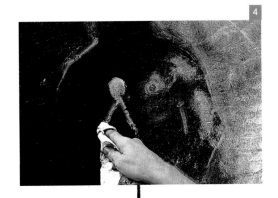

3 Using a paper towel, he applies a clear mixture of half turpentine and half linseed oil to the white paper, coating the entire surface. This mixture keeps the paper wet longer—it will stay wet for approximately four hours. About this technique he says, "Turpentine dries oil paint; linseed oil is the oil in oil paint—half of the mixture I paint with is trying to dry it out, the other is trying to keep it wet—yin and yang—which amuses me no end!"

4 He uses a traditional underpainting technique—in blacks or browns or reds—to get one solid dark color to cover the entire surface. In this case, Arisman uses Mars Black, applied with a paper towel, though a rag would also be fine, in a thin even coat. Then he pulls the whites out with a paper towel. "This process forces two things—you have to be very clear about your light sources and you must work the painting all at one time—you can't get stuck in a corner. This demands simplification. You really have to work a light and dark sketch very clearly beforehand, or you can get lost." Because he's done many figures over time, a sketch is not necessary in this case, but he suggests that his students make sketches until they are more experienced.

A. This is the generic male body, unfinished and just blocked in, with enough light pulled out to indicate its source.

5 On a round table with reference close at hand, Arisman works on the fish shape, which is a cut-out piece of paper. Because he isn't certain of its placement on the man's head, this method gives him freedom to position it later. For illustration, which will be reproduced rather than seen in the original form, a "finish" can contain a great deal of cutting and pasting, giving the artist flexibility, and it saves time. The fish shape is prepared exactly the same way as in Steps 2 and 3, with the white paint and turpentine coating brushed on, then, after it dries, the clear linseed and turpentine mixture applied with a paper towel to keep the surface moist.

4a

5

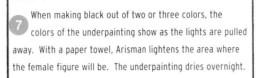
6 Arisman uses the following mixture of colors to achieve the black underpainting of the fish/mermaid: Alizarin Crimson, Ultramarine Blue, Burnt Umber.

7 When making black out of two or three colors, the colors of the underpainting show as the lights are pulled away. With a paper towel, Arisman lightens the area where the female figure will be. The underpainting dries overnight.

8 To the fish's head, he applies runs of pure Naples Yellow and Cadmium Red, using his fingers to paint.

9 His second favorite tool, after his fingers, is the Q-Tip—"it's marvelous." It gives a constant clean surface with which to pull out color, and can be thrown away. Here he uses a Q-Tip to pull out the figure of the mermaid.

10 The form of the fish was overwhelming the form of the woman's body, so with white paint he defines the breasts, arms, and torso. After laying in whites, he emphasizes the breasts and torso with black.

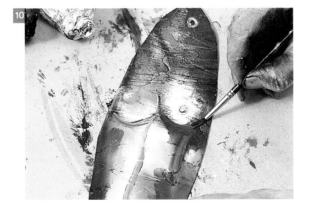

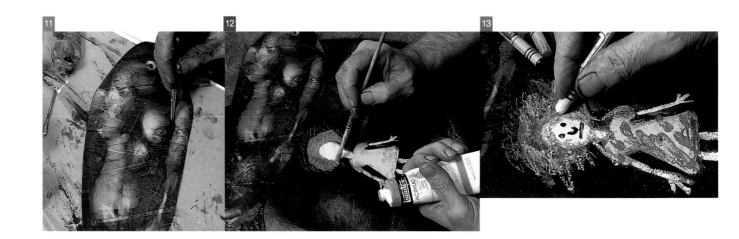

11

Using a small sable brush he finishes painting in the woman's body, which he creates from his imagination. He used a spray adhesive to mount the fish onto the man's head. This is very unstable, but for an illustration that will be reproduced, it is sufficient.

12
One of Arisman's few rules is: Never fake a child's drawing, but in this case, he broke that rule. He would have preferred to have a child do a self-portrait, which he believes is always more convincing.
Another rule: Oil paint can go on top of acrylic, but acrylic cannot go on top of oil. It is very unstable and can be easily scratched off. Again, because it's an illustration for reproduction, he breaks this rule to save time. He uses acrylic Cadmium Orange, Cadmium Yellow and Bleached White to lay out simple child-like shapes.

13
He's added a pattern to the dress, using bright green acrylic paint. Then, he draws in details around the head with Crayola crayons because it's applicable to a child's drawing. But crayon is also very unstable on top of the acrylic paint.

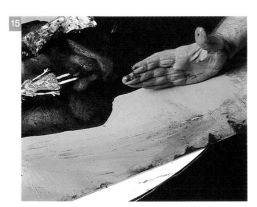

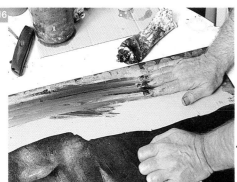

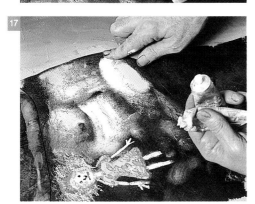

14   With a warm grey oil paint, he paints out the background of the black underpainting to re-form the shape of the man, using a brush to get to the edge of the figure with some control. At this stage he uses good, expensive paint—his preference is Old Holland. The high proportion of pigment to linseed oil gives it more covering power, so he needn't apply more than one coat. It also makes for a kind of lushness for which Arisman's work is known.

15   Once he lays enough oil paint on the figure, rather than take the time to use a brush, he uses his hand to cover the paper with pigment, leveling it out around the figure.
He pulls the paint away from the figure with the flat of his hand. Because his hands are his tools, Arisman cleans them on a rag or, if need be, his pants. When he finishes for the day, he does a final clean-up with turpentine.

16   Having finished the grey background, Arisman decides it looks too graphic, too flat. While it's still wet, he puts more black at the edges then, using his hands, pulls it down through the grey for some tone. This gives a feeling of more light around the figure and that it's drifting into darkness.

17   He says that going back to the Old Masters—Velasquez, Rembrandt, Goya, who also began their paintings with a ground—the theory was that where the light is brightest, the paint is thickest. Because the white in Arisman's underpainting contains some pigment, when white paint goes over it, the result is a middle white. So, it is necessary, as he says, "to clog up in thickness with the lightest and brightest. I'm globbing the white, pushing the whites in." Using Old Holland Flesh, he has also introduced a flesh color so it's not a "ghost body."

18 He's moved the piece off the table and hangs it on the wall again. The man's pants seem to be too black to Arisman, so he adds Hooker's Green.

19 Now, the pants are too green and have made the man look like a surgeon, which is not an element Arisman wants to convey. He mixes inexpensive black and Alizarin Crimson over the green to tone it down.

20 He adds white to pull out the same light source on the pants as he did on the body.

He considers this close to being a finish, but something's missing.

21 He decides it needs yellow—this is not a color theory, he's quick to add—it "just needed it." He fills a brush with Cadmium Yellow, outlines the arm, and the illustration is complete. "Half of the fun of doing illustrations are the accidents that occur in the process. I want to be surprised—which may be bad for business." Here, the mystery of the "mermaid" and the implied presence of the innocent child come together to invoke a disturbing reaction to the idea of adultery.

top "Winged Man," Raw magazine, oil on paper, bottom Serial Killers, Dutton, oil on paper

left "Light Runner," personal work, oil on canvas, 79 x 79 inches, right "Light Runner," personal work, oil on canvas, 38 x 50 inches

top left, "Black Elk," Omni
magazine, oil on paper

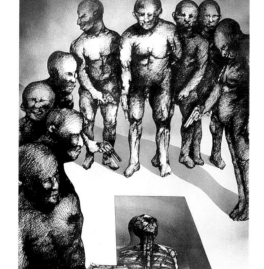

top right, Illustration for article on the use
of bear gall bladders in Asia,
Wildlife Magazine, oil on paper

bottom, "Frozen Images," part of a
series of drawings about violence,
Visual Arts Press, ink and spray paint

Dr. DeMarr by Paul Theroux, Hutchinson Press, collage

marshall
arisman

left, "The Curse of Violent Crime," Time, oil on paper,
right, Heaven Departed, part of a series about the atomic
bomb, Vision Press, Tokyo, oil on paper

marshall
arisman

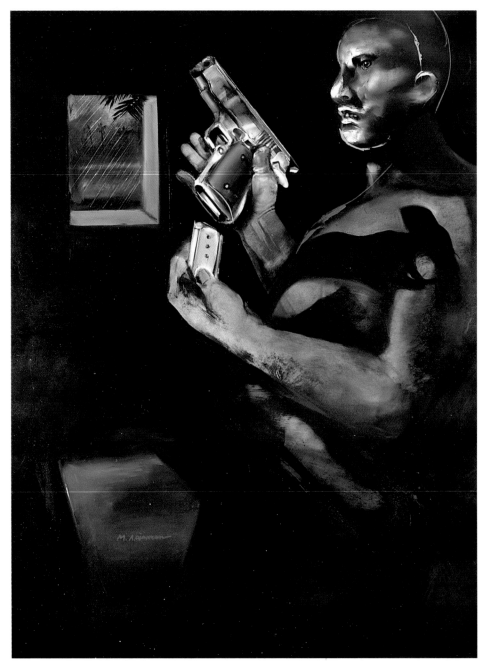

Illustration for an article about an assassin in Vietnam, Playboy, oil on paper

"Reverend Jim Jones," Penthouse, oil on paper

marshall
arisman

"Computerized Man, Omni magazine, oil on paper

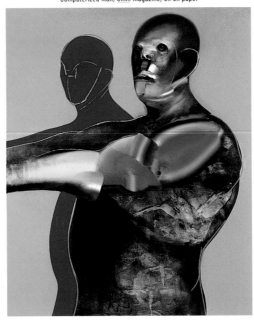

Born and reared in Jamestown, New York,
Marshal Arisman received a fine arts degree from Pratt Institute
in 1960. His illustrations are regularly seen in the Op-Ed page of
The New York Times, The Nation, and Time magazine. He has
received numerous awards from the Society of Illustrators, the
Society of Publication Designers, the American Institute of
Graphic Artists, Graphis Annual, Communication Arts, New York
Art Directors Club, and the Print Casebook Award. A recipient of
the Ida Haskill Award for Study and Travel in Europe, he was also
Playboy's Illustrator of the Year, 1979, and American Artist's
Teacher of the Year, 1994. His work has appeared in many articles and books, and his graphic and fine art in group and one-
man exhibitions. He is represented in the permanent collections
of the Brooklyn Museum, the National Museum of American Art
and the Smithsonian Institute, as well as in many private and
corporate collections. He is Chairman of the Master of Fine Arts
degree program, "Illustration as Visual Essay," at the School of
Visual Arts in New York.

THE ASSIGNMENT:
Because Billout had been married in the not too distant past, and because of his gently humorous, surprisingly philosophical intelligence, he was asked to turn his mind and graphic skills to the concept of "The Wedding." Several calls were made before photography was scheduled—Billout gave assurances that he would be prepared, but failed to mention his "last-minute rule" in the creative process. He had done nothing. Shortly before deadline, a concept sketch was faxed and approved.

THE THOUGHT PROCESS:
Billout considered his own wedding in 1991, quickly discarding the image he had created on the invitations as inappropriate. But he recalled a card he had received at the time titled "Taking the Plunge," a photo of a wedding couple jumping into a swimming pool. He liked the idea of taking a leap, and wanted to use the image of a cliff, one of his favorite landscapes. But he quickly realized that to send newlyweds plunging into a chasm was a rather negative metaphor. So he began making sketches—he has to "draw before he has a concept."

REFERENCE: in addition to the photograph that spurred his imagination, billout used a cliff image which he had already drawn for another job, but had never taken to full finish. he says that sometimes inspiration comes from the material available. brides' magazines gave him the details of the wedding party's clothes.

GUY BILLOUT'S STUDIO IN NEW YORK'S LITTLE ITALY IS LINED WITH FLOOR-TO-CEILING SHELVES OF ART AND REFERENCE BOOKS AND TIERS OF GREEN FILE BOXES. SOME OF THEIR LABELS READ: MACHINES, EASTERN COUNTRIES, NIAGRA FALLS, INDIA, SPAIN, CHILE 1989, ANTARCTICA—A HINT AT BILLOUT'S FASCINATION WITH TRAVEL AND TRANSPORTATION. TWO WALLS OF WINDOWS AFFORD A GREAT VIEW OF LOWER MANHATTAN, AND IN THIS BRIGHT ATMOSPHERE HE TACKLES ASSIGNMENTS AT THE LAST POSSIBLE MOMENT, FINDING THE PRESSURE OF THE TIGHT DEADLINE STIMULATING.

THE STEPS:
Billout's initial inspiration: "Taking the Plunge," a greeting card photo by Kimerbly Guy.

The sketches in the background show how his process of drawing and thinking combine to produce concepts. Discarded ideas include the entire wedding party standing on the train of the bride, or her train becoming a road. Depicting a church, he felt, was a problem, it being too specific. And he'd used the cloud concept too many times, and it was "not dramatic enough, too short of meaning."

Once the process has begun, "the mind is in gear." The idea of the bride's train crossing the chasm came to him in bed, just as he was falling asleep. Finally, he had the positive picture he desired.

At this point he's not sure of the true meaning of the concept—the metaphor of the couple leaving family and friends and going onto an adventure of their own is an interpretation he arrived at later. He considers his work for The Atlantic Monthly to be his best because he is given complete freedom. Without parameters, he never begins from a title or text. Only after the image is complete does he give it a title.

Billout always works to the same size as the reproduction. He makes a black-and-white sketch with a Pilot razor pen and, for the solid black, a dye marker. For him, the cliff has a poetry and drama of its own—without it, the image might have looked banal. He Xeroxes and faxes the sketch for approval.
Very rarely, he's asked to do a color sketch, which he does with dye markers. Once the concept is OK'd, he goes directly to a finish.

4 Using Polaroids of himself for reference, he draws the groom with a Rapidograph. He has also taken a shot of the bride's waving hand gesture.

5 He chooses images from magazines for the bride's and bridesmaids' dresses. He uses reference, even for the tiniest figures. If he makes it up, he feels the drawing tends to be stiff and too humorous—photo reference gives a more serious, realistic look. He traces figures from the magazines. Then, on his copier, he reduces them down (twice on the 200% setting).

6 With a 3HB pencil on tracing paper, he has traced the various elements—the figures and the outline of the cliff—creating a mirror of the final image. He turns the tracing paper over and transfers the drawing onto the final illustration paper by using a burnishing tool—in this case a pair of scissors, which is hard and rounded. The paper is a vellum-finish Bristol, a fine toothed, smooth surface which is flexible, so that scanning for printing is easy.

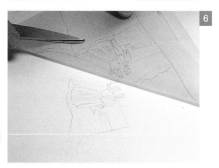

7 A. Having completed the transfer, he has inked in the cliff. Using a light box, he put the vellum over the cliff reference drawing, which is on tracing paper. With a Pilot razor pen, he copied the texture of the cliff. The reference drawing was originally from a photograph. It has been Xeroxed, causing the half tones to drop out, creating a more stylized and dramatic image. Here is the completed black-and-white drawing. To create the solid black, he's covered the finished line drawing with frisket up to where a progression of crosshatching deepens to black, and then airbrushed the area into the chasm. Also, a single tree has been lightly airbrushed with black.

B. Before going to the color finish, he makes a sketch with dye markers on tracing paper over a Xerox of the finished line drawing.

- -

Billout knows he wants a monochromatic treatment and decides upon red and just a bit of violet for the bridesmaids' dresses. Having tried a yellow and red combination, he found it not powerful enough. These days, he's not interested in using an expansive palette. Influenced by the work of painter Mark Tansey, he's found the limited use of color to be very dramatic. Also, there is an old-fashioned aspect to the technique. He recalls that before full-color printing was available, most illustrations were executed in one color plus black, often with very vivid results.

7A

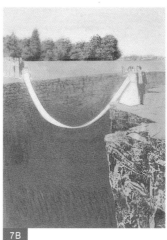

7B

8 A. He applies a low-tack frisket made in England, called "Frisk." Its adhesive quality is not very strong, making it easily removable; also, static electricity holds it to the paper. The cold pressed surface of the vellum has some tooth to it—hot pressed is too smooth and frisket adheres too tenaciously. He removes the cut frisket, uncovering the section to be airbrushed.

B. He cuts with very fine "Ulano" brand blades held in special pen holders. The blades are made in Brooklyn, New York, and are not available in general art supply stores. Cutting masks is, for Billout, like doing "lace work." For large, easy lines, he'll use an X-Acto blade. He airbrushes even the tiniest part of the drawing because it gives a flatness and consistency he can't get doing it by hand. Throughout, he uses a magnifying glass mounted on a lampstand with two lights on either side.

9 His palette: Winsor & Newton watercolors: Winsor Red, Winsor Violet, and two blacks: Lamp Black, a yellowish black which matches the black China ink used in a Rapidograph, and Neutral Tint, a purplish hue, which he uses for the sky.

10 Having put the frisket back down, and using a mixture of Winsor Red and black, he airbrushes the line of trees, building tone from light to dark, working with one color at a time. For protection, he must wear a mask and be in a well-ventilated area. Tissues are constantly used for clean-up.

11 Because of the frisket's smooth surface, it doesn't absorb paint, which can lead to smearing. To speed up the drying process, Billout uses absorbent paper to blot up excess paint and to keep the surface clean.

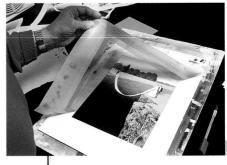

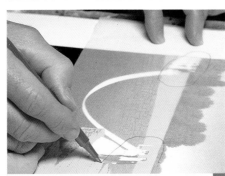

12 He carefully removes the frisket from the sky area. He can reuse the frisket to redo an area, so he saves everything he cuts. They are really "patterns."

13 Airbrushing the sky with the purplish Neutral Tint.

14 He turns the board upside down and rests his hand on paper to keep the drawing clean. Red applied with a #2 sable brush adds some texture to the trees. Because the airbrush gives only a crude delineation of the leaves, the brushwork is necessary to give them a finer outline.

15 To cast the shadow of the bride and groom, he removes the nozzle of the airbrush for a more focused spray.

16 With all painting completed except on the figures themselves, he removes all remaining frisket.

17 To do the tiny work within the figures, he puts tracing paper down over the entire drawing. With a red Pilot pen he indicates where he will cut out "windows" for the small areas where frisket will protect the figures. This gives him a clean surface to work on and uses only a small amount of the expensive "Frisk."

18

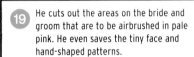

Having cut out frisket to size, he covers the figures within the cut-out tracing paper windows.

19 He cuts out the areas on the bride and groom that are to be airbrushed in pale pink. He even saves the tiny face and hand-shaped patterns.

20 Spraying the faces of the bride and groom using pure Winsor Red.

21 He repeats the steps for the flesh of the wedding party. He draws the maid of honor's bouquet with a red Pilot pen. The Pilot red matches the Winsor Red exactly. This color match makes using the pen for small details faster than using a small brush.

22 He has replaced the tiny patterns that fit the bride and groom's flesh, and has cut out the pants pattern from the frisket. With black, he gives volume to the morning pants, a traditional groom's costume.

23 As he airbrushes shadow and volume into the bridesmaids' dresses using the Neutral Tint, he cuts them out one by one. He must do this in order, left to right, since the shadow is on the right.

It seems like a lot of work, but he's very practiced, so it goes quickly. He feels that he uses the airbrush in a very crude way—very simply, compared to some artists. He uses basic gradations and flat tones.

24 Looking through the magnifying glass, he does some retouching with a Rapidograph.

25 He applies Winsor Violet to the bridesmaids' dresses. Because it's such a small stream of spray, he doesn't wear a mask.

26 He puts his signature on tracing paper and considers its placement. He doesn't want it to be too obvious, or intrusive, or to compete with the idea. On the cliff, it's almost invisible. Because his illustrations tend to be minimalistic, and the visual puns so subtle, the signature can become too important and distracting. "Sometimes the pun is so subtle, the work itself is the signature."

For Billout it is in the creation of the visual that meaning is revealed. And, what is in the mind isn't revealed until he puts it on paper: "You never know unless you have it in a drawing. What you have mentally doesn't always work when it is on paper." Quite clearly, in this case, it works.
He uses FedEx boxes to deliver original work to prevent bending of the illustration. He found that even with many layers of cardboard, messengers and the postal service would find ways to bend the work.

"Works," The Atlantic Monthly, February 1995, Judy Garlan, Art Director

"Panic," <u>The Atlantic Monthly</u>, April 1995, Judy Garlan, Art Director

guy
billout

"Thorns," The Atlantic Monthly, August 1995, Judy Garlan, Art Director

guy
billout

"Salvage," The Atlantic Monthly, February 1996, Judy Garlan, Art Director

"Value," New Jersey Resources Corporation 1994 Annual Report, Michael Gunselman, Art Director

Notebook divider page for Science; for Nike, Inc.; Guido Brouwers, Art Director

"Vision," Le Monde, (France); Saturday, December 30, 1995; Dominique Roynette, Art Director

39

guy
billout

"Ideas," Jefferies Group, Inc.
1995 Annual Report; Douglas Oliver, Art Director

Guy Billout was born in Decize, France, studied advertis-
ing at the Ecole des Arts Appliques de Beaune in
Burgundy, and worked in Parisian ad agencies before
coming to New York in 1969 to become an illustrator. His
work has been published in publications such as New
York, Redbook, McCall's, Glamour, Vogue, Harper's Bazaar,
Playboy, Esquire, Rolling Stone, The New York Times, The
New Republic, The Washington Post Magazine, Money,
Industry Week, Time, Life, Fortune, Discover. Since 1982
Billout has contributed to The Atlantic Monthly in a regu-
lar feature for which he is given total freedom. The same
conditions have recently been granted by the newspaper
Le Monde in Paris. He has received Gold, Silver Medals,
and the Hamilton King Award from the Society of
Illustrators. Selected Illustrator of the Year for the All-
Star Creative Team in Adweek Creativity 1986 issue, he
also received the first prize in an international context
for his 1992 poster for the Seville World's Fair. Four of
Billout's six children's books have been chosen for The
New York Times ten best illustrated children's books.

ALAN COBER'S SPACIOUS HOME
IN SUBURBAN NEW YORK IS FILLED
WITH AN ECLECTIC ARRAY OF ART
AND OBJECTS. HAVING DISPOSED OF
HIS IMPRESSIVE BLACK FOLK ART
COLLECTION, HE HAS BEGUN TO
ACQUIRE PRINTS BY BEN SHAHN,
LEONARD BASKIN, AND THE GERMAN
EXPRESSIONIST ARTISTS. WORKS
BY FELLOW ILLUSTRATORS ARE ALSO
ON DISPLAY. SITUATED ON A GOLF
COURSE, THE QUIET OF COBER'S
STUDIO IS INTERRUPTED ONLY BY
BIRD SONG. THE SKULLS OF A
MOOSE, RAM, ALLIGATOR, STEER, &
SMALLER ANIMALS HANG ON THE
WALLS. BUILT-IN SHELVES HOLD
"32-RUNNING FEET" OF NATIONAL
GEOGRAPHICS FROM 1910 ON,
AS WELL AS REFERENCE BOOKS
AND A LONG ROW OF HIS OWN
SKETCHBOOKS WHICH, IN A WAY,
DOCUMENT HIS ARTISTIC LIFE.

THE ASSIGNMENT:
because Cober's work often
reflects an interest in the
darker areas of the human
psyche, his assignment was
the wrenching topic of
"Divorce." He was given
complete freedom of con-
cept—"short of murder."
The fact that he has had
a long and happy mar-
riage only added to the
challenge. After several
general discussions
by phone, Cober faxed 22
sketches, nearly all of
which were conceptually
interesting. in the meantime, he had
already rejected many of the ideas
and was honing in on the final one.
after further thought and refinement, a
single image was faxed and approved. for
cober, the fax is a mixed blessing. it has
no "hang time, no time to think," and
gives the art director the ability to ask
for one sketch after another. however,
by receiving a manuscript so swiftly, he
gets an extra day to work.

THE THOUGHT PROCESS:

in his early sketches, cober thought he'd tie the couple together with a rope and indicate that it was breaking. but he concluded that if he made the heads and attitudes of the figures mean enough, monstrous enough, the ropes would not be necessary. he began by putting the alligator skull on the woman. for reference, he went to a sketchbook and found a nude he'd done in a drawing class twenty years ago. but he found that having the alligator head on the woman was too extreme and he let it recede. instead, he made the man more blatant: "there's a monster outside; there's a monster inside." he drew the male figure "off the top of his head." he has begun to do this recently, "probably from laziness," though with success. in general, he draws from life, or from polaroids if a model is not available to sit.

At this point he has no ideas about where he'll be using color. He could have chosen to do the woman in color and left the man in black-and-white. "A lot of decisions come from cowardice. Not knowing what to do with her, I left her alone—it's kind of heroic in one sense, but cowardly in another." Ideally, he would have a photograph to work from. "But there wasn't a photograph, or an underdrawing; there wasn't anything. I sit down and start doing it and either I get into trouble or I don't get into trouble." When asked where he gets his ideas—the recurrent themes—he used to say they were just the things that are "around" and didn't have deeper meaning. In recent years, however, he's come to understand that the repetitive themes and interests must have their origins within him: the fascination with skulls, cadavers, dead monkeys, old folks homes, the contents of science museums. In taking some responsibility for his vision, he concedes that its source may be a lot deeper than even he realizes.

THE STEPS:

1 He works on many thumbnail sketches to determine where he's going. This is when the process described above takes place. All 22 sketches were faxed initially, then discussed before a decision was made.

The underlying form is the oval shape which creates three-dimensional volume, key to the
2 success of the overall structure of the final drawing.

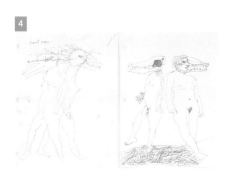

3 As he perfects his ideas, Cober draws directly from the alligator skull. On his work table are the thumbnails and the sketchbook reference of the nude. Because he refers to his own work frequently, he can locate useful images in his sketchbooks with ease.

4 The very rough sketch on the left gave him his final concept. The refined sketch on the right was faxed and approved. Because he'll be drawing on a printing plate, the image on the sketch is reversed on the final print.

5 Cober's method for this piece is dry point on a silicon plate. Wherever a line is drawn, when ink is applied on the plate, it will print, using any etching press. It is a photosensitive, commercial plate used for lithography which comes with a protective film cover to prevent scratching. After he's completed working on the plate, he will send it to a master printmaker in Massachusetts.   Cober uses a stylus to incise the plate. He has a variety of etching tools, but in this case he uses dental tools, some of which he's customized for particular line widths, although he says anything sharp will do.

6 As he works on the plate, he checks to see how the drawing is coming along. After he has painted on it with black India ink using a brush, he rubs off the excess ink with a rag or paper towel so the lines appear. During the printing process, a stiff lithographers ink is rolled over the entire plate with a brayer, a small hand roller used to spread ink thinly and evenly over the plate. The excess ink is rolled off with the same brayer.

7 To give the background texture, he rubs the plate with coarse sandpaper. Initially, he'd thought of making the entire background black, leaving a slight separation between the background and the foreground, but at this point he discards the plan.

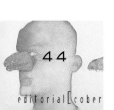

8 The finished plate. This he sends to the printmaker who returns five prints in three days.

9   The print.

10 For color sketches, he makes a series of half-size reductions of the print to the size he's most comfortable working on. At the local copy shop he can control the sizes himself. Because the print is large, he must make copies of each figure separately, which he then pieces together to make a master Xerox. This he duplicates several times. At this point, he might fax the image to an art director, before the color is applied.

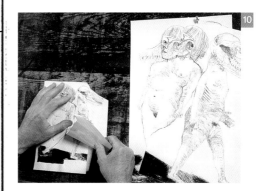

11 He always paints with pan water-colors, using Winsor & Newton or Schmincke paints, applied with Winsor & Newton Series 7 brushes. He has many brass watercolor boxes; this one is a Daniel Smith, with two wells, a thumb hole, and mixing area. He uses these small boxes for all his jobs, on the road, for his sketchbooks, "for the President or the Pope." Although he's been accused of painting directly "out of the tube," he insists that he mixes his colors.

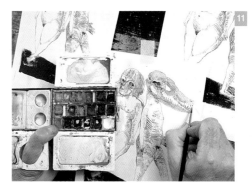

12 He works on a variety of color thumbnails. Determining the color is part of the "unknowing" mentioned earlier—"of the eye knowing or not knowing."

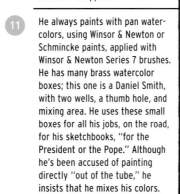

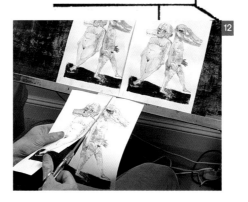

13 Again, Cober considers a totally black background—this time by painting it in. Later, he decides he needs the horizon line and stays with the texture of the print.

14 The final color sketch.

15 Contemplating the original in relation to the color sketches.

16 He begins painting on the print by "fooling around with the teeth, making them bloody."

17 Referring to the sketch, he paints the man inside the skull. He keeps within the line, a skill his artist daughter, Leslie, shares—when she was eight years old she helped Cober color in the loops of the lettering on his illustrations.

18 Working inside the head, he uses a green "mud" color achieved by mixing Aqua and Black. He creates a double image, where the man's teeth become the alligator's.

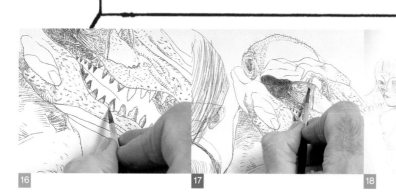

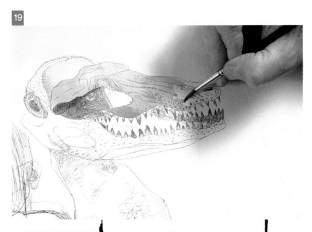

19 To emphasize the man's eye, he uses a touch of Orange, a Bright Red in the corner, Green for the iris, and Yellow for the little band. Here he applies Orange to the skull.

20 At the color sketch stage, he had decided upon the blue body color to contrast the orange skull. Here the hand is painted wet on wet, so it blends with the blue of the body. He flips the print upside down so the color runs up the arm, not down. The man's hands are red so they really pull away from the body color. Also the red makes them look threatening.

21 Two layers of Yellow brighten the inside of the alligator's mouth.

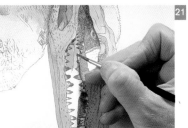

22 To dry the watercolor, he uses a portable hair dryer.

23 With a White Prismacolor pencil, he highlights some of the drawing, so "it turns a little and gives it dimension." This must be done when the watercolor is dry.

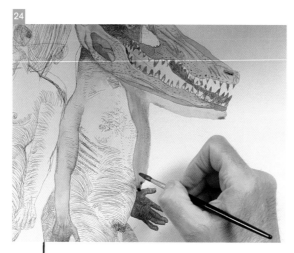

24 The grey color around the man's body was made by using Lamp Black and Blue.

25 Because the background looks too dark and makes the figure appear to be morticed out, Cober goes back with White Prismacolor to lighten the whole tone around the man's body.

26 He draws hairs on the top of the man's head with a graphite pencil.

27 He shades inside the skull with Black Prismacolor to pull it away from the foreground. Crosshatching under the skull and into the grey at the neck also makes this area recede. He has used a white pencil around the teeth to set them off from the background.

28 In the finished illustration, he focused on the penis by leaving it pinkish white, against the bluish body.

Though he barely claims conscious authorship of his ideas, the monstrous emotional revelations of divorce are clear. "I never know what to do, where it's going," he says, "There is no process." He quotes illustrator Mark English who said, "The first ten minutes we're doing art, the rest of the time, we're trying to save it."
Cober puts his final illustrations in a tube or constructs a corrugated package and sends it to clients by FedEx. At this point changes are negotiable in that he can modify the color, but because it is a print, the blacks are final.

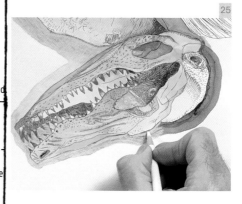

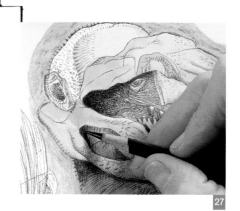

"Ruby Shoots Oswald"
for Texas Monthly magazine's
"150 Moments that Made Texas, Texas,"
watercolor and ink

"The Assassination of Martin Luther King," Skeptic Magazine, 1977

alan e.
cober

left "Pig Nose Man," American Airlines Hemingway Faulkner short story contest winner, drypoint
right "Girl with Boa," American Airlines Hemingway Faulkner short story contest winner, drypoint

Robert McNamara,'' Time magazine, 1995

top "Igor Stravinsky," The Atlantic Monthly, 1982   left "Al Pacino," from "Son of Scarface," Rolling Stone, 1993   right "Joe Louis" Sports Illustrated, unpublished, drawn from life, ink

alan e. cober

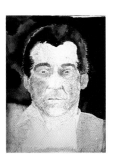

"Willie Pastrano," <u>Sports Illustrated</u>, unpublished, 1980, watercolor, ink, pencil

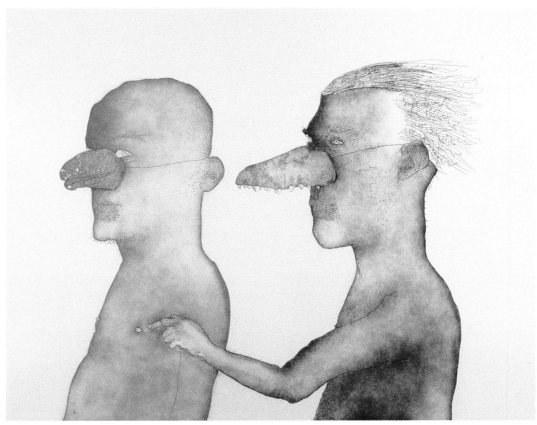

"Mr. Alligator meets Mr. Porpoise," 1993, etching aquatint

alan e.
cober

"The Turner Diaries," The Village Voice Literary Supplement, drypoint

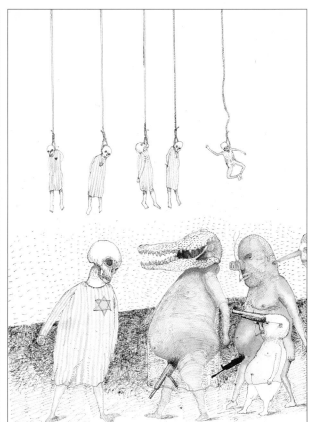

"The Turner Diaries," The Village Voice Literary Supplement, unpublished, drypoint

alan e.
rober

One-man show announcement poster, Art Institute of Boston and the University of Delaware.
From sketchbooks of Saint Maarten, NA; Lake Louise, Albert, CA; Little Tobago, Big Tobago, BVI; The Grand Tetons. Watercolor and ink

alan e.
cober

Born in New York City in 1935, Alan E. Cober is best known for his illustrations in national magazines such as Rolling Stone, The Atlantic Monthly, Time, Newsweek, Life, and Look. Named Distinguished Visiting Artist in Illustration at the State University of New York at Buffalo, and Lamar Dodd Professorial Chair of Art at the University of Georgia, Cober has won numerous awards including medals from the Society of Illustrators and the Art Directors Club of New York. His work is held in the collections of the Library of Congress, the Smithsonian Institution, the New Britain Museum, and the National Air and Space Museum. Included in group and one-man exhibitions, he has shown at the Katonah Museum of Art, Burchfield Art Center, Buffalo State College, University Gallery and University of Delaware, among others. His book, The Forgotten Society, reveals the life of the patients at the Willowbrook State Institution for the Retarded, inmates at Sing Sing prison, and the aged and dying in a rest home.

THE ASSIGNMENT:

duillo has been providing romantic images for magazines and books for thirty years—she was a natural choice for the "Love" theme. When she was contacted for the project she was at work on the jacket art for a book entitled Shadows and Lace by Teresa Medeiros for Art Director Yook Louie at Bantam Books. The assignment was ideal for the romantic theme of our project, and without some of the specific problems of book work—no wraparound art and no areas left open for for type consideration. Her husband, John Duillo, an illustrator and former professional photographer, chronicled her progress.

IN AN UNPRETENTIOUS HOUSE ON A QUIET STREET IN HICKSVILLE, NEW YORK, ELAINE DUILLO WORKS IN AN UPSTAIRS STUDIO UNDER A SKY-LIGHT. EXAMPLES OF HER LONG, AWARD-FILLED CAREER ARE IN EVI-DENCE—LUMINOUS PAINTINGS OF HANDSOME MEN AND BEAUTIFUL WOMEN IN PERIOD COSTUMES, OR NEARLY UNCLOTHED, PASSIONATELY EMBRACING. THE WORKS ARE METIC-ULOUSLY PAINTED, WITH ATTENTION TO THE ENTIRE PICTURE SURFACE, NOT ONLY TO THE CREAMY COMPLEX-IONS AND MASCULINE BUILDS OF THE CHARACTERS PORTRAYED.

THE THOUGHT PROCESS: *duillo received from the publisher an information sheet about the book: setting: medieval england 1298; characters: heroine, blue-eyed rowena fordyce, a "wheaten blond, with long and wavy hair as though recently removed from braids. hero: gareth decre-cy, the dark lord of caerleon, with 'deep velvety brown' eyes, and wavy dark hair."*

duillo wanted to create a romanticized version of love and courtship in the twelfth century, a fantasy: the damsel and her knight. her goal was to make "the heroine vulnerable, but with a feeling of strength. the hero must appear powerful and tender at the same time. they would have to relate to each other in a serious and truly meaningful way."

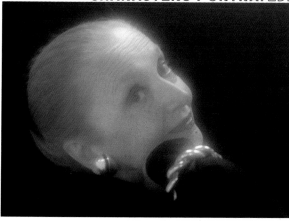

1

THE STEPS: Models and costumes are assembled at a photographer's studio geared to an illustrator's needs and concerns. In this case, no pre-sketches were made because Duillo knew exactly in what direction she intended to go and what lighting was needed. Duillo hired a fair-haired, delicate model, and the photographer had the appropriate costume. Accuracy within a hundred years is all that's required for this type of work. The knight's costume was rented from a special collection of military dress. The information sheet indicated that "armor was not the full metal of later years, but was a mixture of leather and chain mail." The chain mail is crocheted; the real thing would be too bulky for a close embrace.

The photographer shoots six to eight rolls as Duillo helps out in directing the pose and lighting. From contact sheets and negatives her husband makes prints. She uses black-and-white photos for reference and never shoots in color. In this way, she's not "held hostage by the colors of the photos." She uses the lightest exposure and prefers a print smaller than the standard 11" by 14". She has it printed in two parts so she can hold it close to see into the shadows.

To see the hands properly, she taped the photos together.

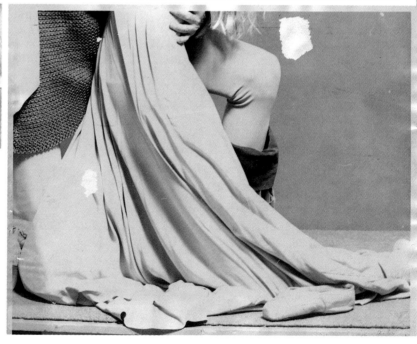

2 She makes a fairly accurate black-and-white sketch with 2H and HB pencils which she scumbles with her finger or a stub, to show the art director and the editor. She presents one solitary sketch for approval and possible changes from the A.D., and a final "go ahead," from the editor. In the past, she would make three full-color sketches, but found that editors might pick elements from each of the three, necessitating another new and dynamic design.
This sketch, based on the photograph, took two days to complete. She gave her hero a beard to make him a less callow youth than the model. Editorial requests had included a stained glass design and wild flowers, as background, and three small medieval castles. She only created two, without reference, since they needed little detail. She's frequently had to illustrate castles and has used reference from Scotch whiskey advertisements, as well as from the library and her own extensive files.
At this stage she knows the eventual cropping for the final illustration.

3 The art director eliminated one castle and changed the value system on the heroine's dress for a better flow of the light value in the illustration. Duillo always tries to have good light and dark movement in her illustration and welcomed this change. Corrections and restrictions sometimes have a very positive effect on the artist in the way of growth and expansion of the thought process. Without challenge, an illustrator working in the romance genre can become bored and stale. Duillo uses acrylics, so when the paint goes down on the board, it dries almost immediately. Consequently, she tries to get all changes from the publishers at the sketch stage, as changes on the finish are nearly impossible, unless she's painting something "out."

4 Using a Beloptican—a kind of opaque projector, she projects the sketch directly on uncoated, medium cold pressed Crescent illustration board. She tries to incorporate the concepts of negative space, a good dark and light movement and overall solid design in her work—as the stained glass behind the figures shows. She puts a great deal of thought and planning into her illustrations—her aim is "to make the romance genre credible in every way, when it concerns art and craftsmanship."
Here she begins with an opaque black outline of the stained glass, working around both figures to achieve balance.

5

She uses acrylic paint with water—no medium, no retarder, no gels. She always uses the Raphael 8404 Maitre Kolinsky #5 brush, an expensive brush manu-factured in France. On occasion she uses Prismacolor pencils to save time, as they take the place of an opaque value.

She purchases her paints in tubes and puts as much as needed in small jars—her original Liquetex jars from 1959. She puts a small amount of water in each jar and mixes part of the paint with that water. In this manner, she has paint that can be used for thin glazes and the remainder for more opaque washes.

The hue and value of the paint depends on how much of the stark white of the illustration board shows through—the key to the luminosity for which her work is known. The acrylics produce a luminosity which can't be duplicated with oils, although, she says, the brightness of color necessary for reproduction may not be what would be considered acceptable for "gallery work."

A. She completes the stained glass design. To reproduce properly, she may have to paint several lay-ers of the opaque colors she often uses in her back-grounds, so that streaks don't show.

6 Here she "pins down the hair," because she'll be putting the background behind her hero. When she does a wraparound cover, she starts on the back page to "warm up," but this illustration has a relatively simple focus.

7 Duillo pre-mixes a special color, a burgundy she calls "wine," which is made of Dioxazine Purple, Pthalo Blue, and Aqua Violet. She uses this for his hair, com-bined with another of her pre-mixed colors, a rich dark green: Hookers Green, Pthalocyanine Blue, Dioxazine Purple. Black does not reproduce well on paperbacks because of the cheap printing, so it should be avoided in any transparent wash. She also com-pletes the darks of the man's figure.

8 She paints around the light areas of the hair and some of the wild flowers. The red for background is made up of Naphthol Red Light overlaid with Alizarin Crimson. The red must be layered several times and for the landscape area, some white is added to take down the intensity of the hue.

For the large, uninterrupted washes of the translucent stained glass window, she uses a Longnickel 3000 Combo #20 brush, after she's edged around with the smaller French brush. These are the only two brushes she uses and are her most expensive tools. The repetitive edging around the hair and figures is a "tedious process and not for the fainthearted or those artists interested in making a fast buck!"

5

5a

6

7

8

9

The lower left corner is begun, continuing the enclosure of the figures. She exaggerates the size of flowers found in a seed catalogue and "makes the rest up." To show spacial relation, she has to push the daisies back by adding a darker wash over the area.

10

She paints in the man's face and chain mail, starting with the darks—a black she mixes using greens, blues and purples. Duillo does not use a formula for any of her colors, but while she's "concentrating on the painting, she mushes them around the palette."

11

A detail of the man's skin tone is created with several washes of Acra Red and Raw Umber, which she then cools with a medium-value green, making adjustments as she works.

The man's head alone takes a full day to paint. All the highlights on his armor and hair are areas where there is only a very light wash so the white of the illustration board shows through.

12

Duillo creates the flesh color of the woman's hands by using Raw Umber, Acra Violet, Brilliant Yellow Green in very pale washes, building up value from light to dark as she goes.

For her damsel's face, she starts with the area under the chin. She paints in the value as it appears in the light black-and-white photograph, because she may not want it darker. She can add if she wants, but she cannot subtract. The shadows are Raw Umber, sometimes Yellow and Acra Red. To deepen it she adds Bright Orange. For the darker shadows she uses Pthalocyanine Blue and Umber. The last, darkest shadow is made with the premixed "wine." The stained glass color behind the knight's shoulder is created with "wine" with a tiny drop of Naphtol Red Light and Indo Orange Red—all in a very thin wash.

For the hair, a very pale mix of a Raw Umber and Cadmium Yellow Medium are washed over the white of the board. She counsels that the background must be brought into the figures—even subtly—so that the figures don't appear to be cut-outs.

The directive from the information sheet regarding the dress was: "a simple, colorful sleeveless shift over long-sleeved undertunic. Ignore the title when costuming the characters. There was no lace in medieval times." The dress is "wine," thinned out with straight Dioxazine Purple to give it a pinker hue, and put on in a pale wash. There are areas in the dress that are almost white. By this time she has added, still without reference, tighter details of the castle.

Usually when Duillo works, she covers the heads as they are completed, using paper or whatever's lying around. "God forbid something should happen to the heads!"

17 She draws in the lines of the dress first so she doesn't lose the drawing. To protect the painting beneath, she rests her hand on a piece of paper.

18 She lays down the lightest wash all over the gown area, building up the value system until she gets to the darkest. She applies six or eight washes to create the lavender and violet of the dress, which takes the whole day.

19 In this close-up of completed lower dress she uses Prismacolor for opacity. For the petals of the daisies, she applies the thinnest and palest yellow wash over the white illustration board. For the foliage, she splays a brush filled with a mix of green pigment, "sees what it looks like," then adds patterns. "That's the fun part, watching the colors blend—and it's different every time."

20 Her drawing board bears the legend: "Sanity is the playground of the uncreative." Here we see her work area with the enamel pan she uses for mixing paints. Although she has reconstructed the colors she used for this job, in fact, she uses her colors by instinct, saying "whatever's in the jar." It's a "discovery" for her.

The final piece, painstakingly executed—took Duillo ten full days at the board, and accomplished what she set out to do—portray a powerful yet sensitive 12th century knight and his vulnerable damsel. "The excitement is getting in there with the paint and seeing what happens."
She FedExes her work, carefully packaged, though she prefers delivering the job in person to get a reaction from the art director.

Geisha Diary, Berkley Books

elaine
duillo

top <u>This Place to Honor</u>, Bantam Books, left <u>Sketch for Duchess</u>, Warner Books, right Love's <u>Glittering Web</u>, Harlequin

Song of the Seabird, Harlequin

elaine
duillo

top Cherish the Dream, Dell Publishing Company, bottom Golden Roses, Avon Books

top left One Sunny Day, Berkely Books, top right Adventure Train, Warner Books
bottom left Defy Not the Heart, Avon Books, bottom right Perfect Circles, Berkley Books

elaine
duillo

top <u>Drums of Time</u>, Ballantine Books, bottom <u>This Cruel Beauty</u>, Avon Books

elaine
duillo

Keeper of the Dream, Dell Publishing Company

elaine
duillo

At the High School of Music and Art in New York, Elaine Duillo was a classmate of the future illustration stars, Daniel Schwartz, Burt Silverman, and Harvey Dinnerstein. She went on to Pratt Institute and began a career that took her from depicting adventure, mystery, and gothics, to painting historical romance novels for publishers around the world. Many authors and publishers depend on Duillo to help put their books on the best seller lists, including that of The New York Times. In June 1989, she capped a thirty-year career with a major retrospective at the Society of Illustrators. Her work has been represented in the Pratt 100 Year Salute Show, the Society of Illustrators Annual Exhibitions and Paperback Shows. She received the Romantic Times Award for Illustrators, was featured in People magazine, and appeared on Fox TV and the Geraldo Rivera Show. Her work has been in group shows nationwide and hangs in many private collections.

top The Poe Papers, Berkley Jove, bottom Enchantress Mine, Signet

—and she is learning to work digitally— she prefers the hands-on method. What she'll be losing most by going to computer is the tactile, sensual part of the art where the artist handles the paper, cuts with scissors, and applies rubber cement.

"There's something about being able to handle the material that is not the same as pushing a mouse around." She describes the delight of being in a sunny room surrounded by the visuals she's working on, as opposed to working at the computer in the dark looking at a screen. To her, there's something very cloistered about the process. However, the principles of her technique remain the same, whether applied to hands-on or to computer manipulation.

Color, composition, aesthetic judgement—all the artistic skills and talents—are necessary to create a good illustration.   Her theory about the current popularity of collage is

COLLAGE HAS ALWAYS INTRIGUED JOAN HALL. FROM HER EARLY CHILD-HOOD SHE NOT ONLY CUT OUT PAPER DOLLS—SHE WAS FASCINATED WITH EPHEMERA AND DIFFERENT KINDS OF NOSTALGIA. HER STUDIO, WITH ITS WIDE, OPEN VIEW OF MANHATTAN, IS CROWDED WITH OAK FLAT FILES FROM THE TURN OF THE CENTURY. THEY'RE FILLED WITH ART SUPPLIES, POSTCARDS, DOILIES AND LACE, FANCY PUSHPINS, ANTIQUE VALENTINES, DECORATIONS, AND STICKERS, SUCH AS FISH AND MUSICAL NOTES. MOST SURFACES HAVE ARTFULLY-ARRANGED FOUND-OBJECTS, A COLLEC-TION THAT INCLUDES FOSSILS, A PAIR OF SHAKING HANDS, MEDALS, A BROKEN BAL-LERINA, SHELLS THAT LOOK LIKE DINOSAURS, AND A PRE-COLUMBIAN PIECE GIVEN TO HER BY A FRIEND. LIKE MANY OTHERS, HALL FEELS THE WHOLE INDUSTRY IS CHANGING BECAUSE OF THE COMPUTER. ALTHOUGH SHE CONSIDERS IT A GOOD TOOL

that because we live with such a fast, on-the-run mentality, we respond to the look of spontaneity and quickness in a collage. like graffiti, it's a sociological expres-sion of our times. and, in fact, it can be very quickly executed; with her experience and resources, she can produce a fin-ished illustration in a day. **the assignment:** hall's initial assign-ment was "the history of love," which, after some discussion, became more generalized. for an historical overview, wherein a vari-ety of couples would symbolize a march through time, contemporary images would be needed. this created a problem with usage of contemporary photographs, since there was no budget for useage fees. because our assignment could be more flexible, hall took on a more overall statement of love.

THE THOUGHT PROCESS: *when considering such an open statement as love, hall says, "it's a biggie; i thought about it for several days. i wanted to depict it as spiritual love—not necessarily romantic love—but overall love, love of mankind. the more i thought about it, the more i realized it was too difficult for this assignment. so i had to think, 'what do i think of love?' what came more naturally to me was something sarcastic and humorous. the concept came to me to show different kinds of human love depicted through various couples. i wanted to represent both heterosexual and homosexual love. i wanted to show the adam and eve symbol in which the apples on the tree of knowledge were changed to hearts. i also wanted the romantic, idyllic, and poetic, and finally, something extremely blase and ho-hum. the bouquet could be fun as both phallic and a female. i saw a disapproving sun as a parental symbol. the overall feeling was that of the landscape as a scrim or stage set. behind the scene, thunder and lightning is lurking; the dark side is revealed by cherubs. in love, you don't have just the positive and the good and the romantic. even when you do, how long does that last? i didn't want to be negative, but rather to show both things. the predominant image is positive. that's the way i see it, so although it looks like a surrealistic scene, to me it is super real."* because her sketch is *almost a finish,* hall gets approval for the concept from the client before she even begins doing research. this is the point where changes occur, at the art director's or editor's suggestion.

RESEARCH: Sometimes clients will supply material they want her to use, which she likes, if it's better than what she has. It is always appreciated when the art director works closely with the artist.

Hall has extensive photo and art files, clearly labeled. In addition to the expected categories of Animals, Famous People, Sports, and Travel, here is a sample of the kinds of things a collage artist needs: Archeology—Fossils and Shells; Bathroom Stuff; Bicycles; Carnivals; Cartoons; Christmas Stuff; Cities—American Future; Cosmetics; Crime; Electricity; Fairs; Footwear; Household Goods; Humor; Locks and Keys; Maps; Medical & Dental; Money; Narcotics; Nudes; People—Crowds, Parties, Faces, Men and Women, Modern Babies, Classical People, Ethnic People, People—Overweight Modern, People—Sleeping or Relaxing, Famous Political People; Presidents; Protestors; Royalty; Signs and Symbols; Snow; Space Travel; Supernatural Magic; Telephones; Tools and Instruments, Toys, Wars and Weapons. Copyright is also a concern, but Hall has never had problems because she has always used images which are in the public domain or are significantly changed, so there is no copyright infringement. She admits it's difficult to keep up-to-date with the rapidly changing copyright laws. With the classical images she used for this assignment, she called Art Resource—a fine art photo archive and rights and permissions representative in North America for a variety of museums and archives—to check that the images were free to use. Anyone doing collage for reproduction should be aware that they must check for the feasibility of use. Sometimes fees must be paid for usage—it's part of the expense of doing the job.

In addition to her extensive files, Hall uses the New York Public Library's Picture Collection because the resolution of many of her older pieces isn't always clean. She gets color laser copies made of the images from the Library. From her own files she gleaned imagery from the following categories: Electricity, Classic Women and Children, and Sunrises and Sunsets (Rainbows, Clouds). In choosing the source material she must eliminate from a large number of possibilities. Here she considers various groupings.

1 THE STEPS

2 She assembles items of interest from the various sources of research. At this point she's chosen all the images for the illustration. Then, she experiments with the colored items until she is satisfied, envisioning how it will look later in scale.

3 To get the proper scale, she uses a percentage wheel by measuring the original and the size she wants it to be. The obvious scales she knows from experience: 100% is same size, 50% is half, 200% is twice. But if she needs a tight percentage, she uses the wheel. Then she does black-and-white Xeroxing on her home machine and labels the amount of reduction on the back. In this case, the image is 80% of the original.

4 Hall uses a pair of sewing scissors which she bought in Paris years ago to cut out the black-and-white Xeroxes. Her favorite tool, the scissors are beautiful to look at and "feel so good." She has a professional sharpen her scissors.

5 She must carefully cut out the woman's fingers which will be silhouetted. To her, the skill of cutting is like the skill of drawing and takes the same kind of hand/eye coordination.

6 On a self-healing cutting board, she uses an X-Acto blade for straight edges.

7 Here Hall assembles the cut-out black-and-white Xeroxes into a collage.

76

8 Using Scotch Removable Magic Tape No. 811, she tacks down the black-and-white collage. The tape allows for the Xerox to be put down temporarily and if necessary, lifted up without damage. This way, she needn't commit herself to gluing until she's satisfied with the composition.

9 She pencils in the lines which had faded in the Xerox.

10 This is the 80% reduction of the Xerox of the final black-and-white collage—the sketch. She faxes it to the client for approval, which she receives.

11 In a local copy shop, she gets the color laser prints of the images enlarged or reduced to the sizes she's determined in the black-and-white sketch. She's found that the Color Laser 800 is very sharp and is also reasonably priced. She usually gets more than one copy, in case of error, or if she likes the image and wishes to keep it on file. These she stores without cutting them out, otherwise the edges get "dog-eared."   She cuts out each image and compares it with the black-and-white Xerox for size.

12 With markers, she disguises the white edges where cuts have been made, to prevent them from showing in reproduction. She matches the color, or goes slightly darker, using permanent markers which do not bleed into the image and will not smear when rubber cement is applied. She prefers a wide-tip marker for easy manipulation.

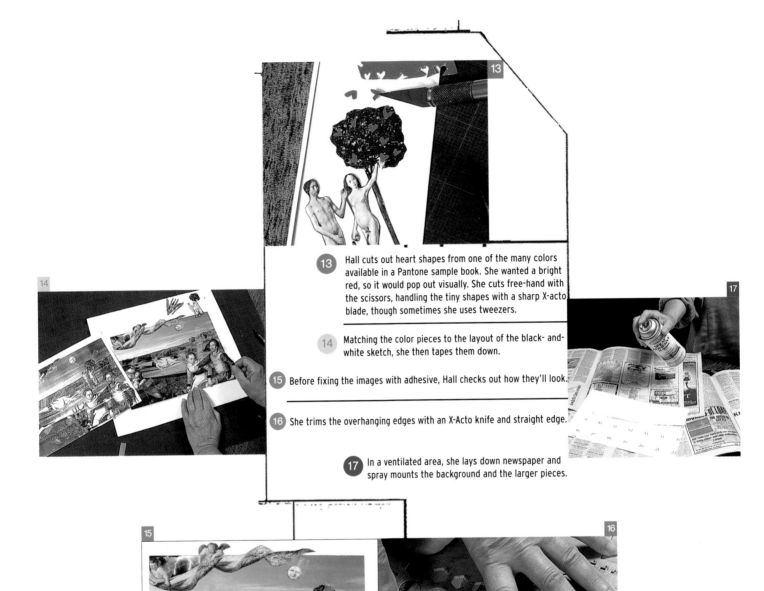

13 Hall cuts out heart shapes from one of the many colors available in a Pantone sample book. She wanted a bright red, so it would pop out visually. She cuts free-hand with the scissors, handling the tiny shapes with a sharp X-acto blade, though sometimes she uses tweezers.

14 Matching the color pieces to the layout of the black- and white sketch, she then tapes them down.

15 Before fixing the images with adhesive, Hall checks out how they'll look.

16 She trims the overhanging edges with an X-Acto knife and straight edge.

17 In a ventilated area, she lays down newspaper and spray mounts the background and the larger pieces.

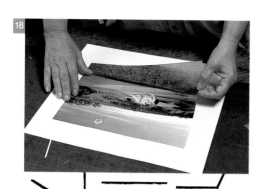

18 The pieces are mounted onto white pliable illustration board—the flexibility is necessary for when the piece is bent around the scanner drum by the printer for film separation.

19 Protecting the image with tracing paper, she uses a roller to insure adherence.

20 For the smaller images, she applies rubber cement, which can be lifted with thinner if changes are required. But rubber cement is not permanent and tends to yellow over time.

21 There are times when she uses an archival, permanent fine art glue, called Yes. It's acid free and thicker so it won't buckle, but it's not removable, so changes can't be made.

22 She cleans the excess rubber cement using thinner on a Q-tip. Or a rubber cement pick-up.

23 With Eagle Prismacolor pencils she touches up where cut lines were missed, or where she wants to brighten or intensify an area, or to shade if necessary.

24 Hall decides on a last minute change in the sky area. Looking at the whole color image, she doesn't feel right about the drapery—it seems as though the cherubs are flying with a rug or curtain. It doesn't read as the sky being peeled back to reveal the storm. She decides to make the sky look more like a page turning. Using a Pantone graduated paper to match the blue of the sky background, she cuts it out with an X-Acto knife against a plastic French Curve. She pastes down the substitute sky.

25 With a purple pencil, she gives more definition to the shadow that's been created with the Pantone paper.

26 For presentation, Hall uses a rubber stamp logo with her address. A tissue cut to size goes over the piece to protect it—she feels it's a nice way to present it—and this is how it goes to the art director.
If there should be a problem, the client returns the original and Hall discusses the validity of any change. Sometimes a suggestion is made which she agrees will improve the piece, and using rubber cement liquid thinner, she makes the changes. This is a rare occurrence.

Although the final illustration is no longer an historical overview of love, it does take in a large array of romantic possibilities. And it has that extra depth unimagined when the assignment was given—that "behind love there is always this other thing." The artist always invests the work with his or her own point of view. As Hall says, "It's a personal statement. It has to be, how can you take yourself out of your art?" Hall spent time performing as a mime, another art form of wordless communication, and she feels it has carried over to her collages and is reflected in the surrealistic way she works. She says, "What goes into the life of the artist is translated into the art."

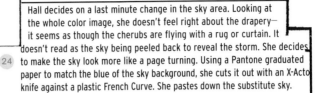

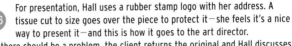

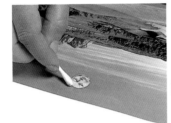

22

23

24

25

26

"Wall Street," Information Week

81

joan
hall

"My Diet," The New York Times Magazine

joan
hall

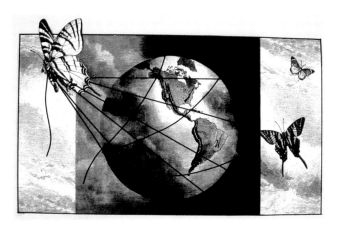

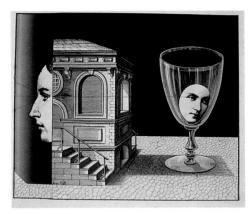

Four editorial pieces, The New York Times

joan
hall

"A Voyage Through Time, Space and Your Head," Follett Library

"Kobe Earthquake," Bloomberg Magazine

top "If You Could Dine Anywhere," Gourmet Magazine, Carte Blanche   bottom "Derryll" Tape jacket for demo

"Adult Education," New York magazine

A native New Yorker, Joan Hall attended the Juilliard School of Music, apprenticed with Anthony Grey in London, and attended the Insituto de Allende in Mexico. Her illustrations have appeared in prestigious magazines including Time, Life, The Atlantic Monthly, The New York Times, and TV Guide, and she's worked for many publishers and advertising agencies. Examples of her work have appeared in over 45 books about art, illustration, and three-dimensional work. She has exhibited her work in group exhibitions at the Society of Illustrators, where she has been accepted into many of their Annual Exhibitions; at the Art Directors Club of New York; Museo Rufino Tomayo, Mexico City; and the Centre Cultural Georges Pompidou, Paris, France. She's held one-person shows at the South Street Seaport Museum in New York; the American Cultural Centers, United States Information Service in Brasilia – where she also held seminars – New Delhi, and Paris. She has taught at the School of Visual Arts from 1978 to the present.

WITH A VIEW OF THE LUSH
GARDEN AND SWIMMING POOL OF
HIS HOME IN SOUTHAMPTON, LONG
ISLAND, WILSON MCLEAN WORKS AT
HIS EASEL IN A NEWLY CONSTRUCTED
STUDIO. AFTER 27 YEARS IN NEW
YORK CITY, HE MOVED FULL TIME TO
HIS SHINGLED HOUSE IN ARTISTS
VILLAGE, WHERE THE IMPRESSIONIST
PAINTER WILLIAM MERRITT CHASE
HAD A SUMMER ART COLONY AT THE
TURN OF THE CENTURY. LIGHT FROM A
BANK OF FRENCH DOORS AND SKY-
LIGHTS FILLS THE HIGH-CEILINGED
ROOM WHERE A COLLECTION OF
AFRICAN MASKS AND ANTIQUE WOOD-
EN HAT MOLDS SHARE SPACE WITH
MCLEAN'S LARGE CANVASES—ILLUS-
TRATIONS AND PERSONAL WORK.

THE ASSIGNMENT:
After some discussion about his topic, McLean focused on "Fantasy" as a general subject.
Although he is not known for female figures, this was an opportunity to imagine a "challanging, idealized woman you could lust after who would also be cruel."

THE THOUGHT PROCESS: McLean envisioned "an Ava Gardner type, a woman who could trounce you, but it would be wonderful agony. She could crunch you but you'd be smiling all the way to your death." The bird sybolizes gentleness, *and the snake is sensual, cruel, and an "obviously" male symbol that she sensually caresses. he liked the monumentality of the female figure, which he drew without reference. he deliberately exaggerated the proportions, making broad shoulders and hips and a small head to give her an idealized amazonian feeling. there was a sense of looking up at the woman, which also evokes her power. he used reference from his own library and scrap to sketch in the orchid, bird, and snake.*

WILSON McLEAN 90

THE STEPS:

1 The sketch on the left was faxed for approval. At the time the project was scheduled to begin, McLean was unable to get a model to photograph for reference. But because his sketch pleased him, he decided to go ahead without photographic reference. Working directly from the sketch, he draws on the canvas with a 3H pencil. He invents her left hand with the bird, but it doesn't seem totally convincing. He does not attempt to draw the hand touching the snake without reference. The woman's hair began as a smaller shape, following the neckline in a Belle Epoque hair-do. He felt the composition needed weight and contrast to the small head, so he sent the hair sailing out. He works on a 30-by 20-inch prepared, oil-gessoed, double-linen canvas, which he stretches himself on a heavy duty stretcher. His lighting is a combination of a balance-corrected tungsten daylight fluorescent bulb and a Veralux full-spectrum lamp.

2 After the simple line drawing has been completed, McLean begins to fill in the background underpainting in a deep reddish brown created by mixing Titanium White, English Red Deep, Burnt Sienna, Indian Red, Chrome Green, and Flesh Tint. It should be noted that McLean mixes varying amounts of Titaniaum White with ALL his colors for opacity. He never does washes or glazes. He uses a one-inch flat sable oil brush and, for scumbling, a half-inch, round filbert white bristle brush. He smooths things out with a #6 sable brush. The hair, which is slightly darker than the underpainting, he created with a palette knife.
A. McLean uses a variety of brands, such as Old Holland and Winsor & Newton, piled on a large table near the easel. Because of his complex and subtle use of color, he chooses his pigments by hue, not brand.
B. His palette is a large piece of glass for laying out the paints and mixing.

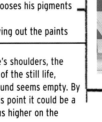

3 Because of the flat horizon behind the figure's shoulders, the vertical space around her, and all the action of the still life, snake and flower at the bottom, the background seems empty. By creating the square shape behind her—at this point it could be a table, a tablecloth or a cube—he throws focus higher on the torso, and breaks up the horizon line.

4 He makes a subtle change in the background color up to the horizon line. The overpainting color is a mix of White, French Ultramarine Blue, Scheveningen Blue Light, Kings Blue Light, Naples Yellow, Permanent Green Middle, and Dioxene Purple. To get a texture, he puts the paint on with a palette knife.

5 For the underpainting of the chair he mixes White, Indian Red, Black, Vandyke Brown, Yellow Ochre Pale, Dioxene Purple, Winsor Violet, and Mixed Green Light.
He's using reference for the body of the snake from one of his books, but needs a better head. He partially paints in the snake's red stripe, mixing Cadmium Red Deep, Scheveningen Violet, and Scheveningen Red. The blue is French Ultramarine Blue, Indian Red, and Cobalt Blue where it is lighter.

6 At this stage, McLean notes that the chair, snake, and background are rather monochromatic—similar in coloration and value. He adds the blue horizontal band, the first really different color in the illustration. First, he mixes French Ultramarine and Cobalt Blue with White. Then, to mottle the texture, he adds Indian Red on top with a bristle brush so it "scratches its way through to the blue."
He adds the snake's yellow bands with a mix of Cadmium Yellow, Cadmium Yellow Deep, and Lemon Yellow Hue.
He considers painting the orchid white because the reference for the petals of this particular orchid indicates white, but decides to go with a pinky red for aesthetic reasons.

7 To get the head and hand reference, his wife, Rosemary Howard, a former fashion photographer, took pictures of a model. Because McLean was not present at the shoot, neither the head nor body were at the correct angle. Preferring his sketch, he stuck with it for the finish, but the model's hands were just what he needed. From 35mm color slides, he had photocopies blown up.

8 He lays in the deep, dark underpainting indicating the shadow down the right-hand side of the body, establishing the light source on the left. Pigments used for the underpainting are: Vandyke Brown, Indian Red, Hooker's Green, Deep Lake, Cadmium Red Deep, Burnt Sienna, Mauve, and Naples Yellow.

9 Laying in lighter tones, he fills in the thighs using White, Bright Red, Hooker's Green Lake Deep, Cadmium Yellow Pale, Indian Red, Purple, Manganese Violet Blue, Naples Yellow Reddish Extra, and Lead Red Hue.

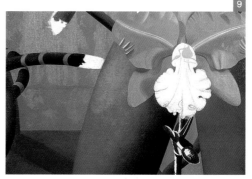

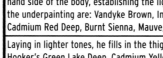

10

Because he works with opaque colors and not glazes, McLean works from dark to light throughout, now filling in the torso.

11 Now with good reference, he sketches in the left hand which touches the snake.

To finish the arm and hand and to get the ultimately smooth skin surface for which he is known, he uses #3 Isabey sable watercolor brushes—the equivalent of the more standard #2 (like Winsor & Newton). Although sable brushes are easily used up on canvas, bristle brushes are too rough to achieve the desired softness of the skin.

12

13

The color of the bird is "a total lie." McLean's reference material was a plain, brown bird—a portion of which can be see in the lower center of Step 1—but the angle, size and shape was what was needed. So he invented the colors, using Prussian Blue, Scheveningen Blue Light, Pthalo Turquoise, Purple, Rose Madder Lake, Naples Yellow, Reddish Extra. For details he works with a #2 Isabey brush, (the equivalent of a #1 Winsor & Newton brush).
A. Having put the darks in first, he paints dark to light. This way he can relate the darks of the torso to the darks of the bird.
B. A detail of the bird, not yet finished.

The orchid reference is from gardening magazines and an orchid book he had on hand. He took the shape of the petals from one source and the stamen, which was "sexier," from another. The pink color is two or three deep reds plus White and the stamen is Cadmium Yellow and Chinese Orange.

To begin work on the face, he uses magazine reference of faces that are at a similar angle: a small image of the opera diva Jessie Norman that indicated shadows well, and one of a model in an advertisement. He sketches in the blank area of the head in detail, using a #3H pencil on the canvas.

He paints from dark to light and blocks in the head. But at this point he feels the woman is a bit mannish and hard. The challenge will be to turn the face into something more pleasing. He then goes on to finish the smooth skin tones of the rest of the figure.

McLean arranges the canvas to the correct height on his large easel by building up stretchers under it. Years ago, he built a "hand guide" to rest on while doing detail work. The hand guide resembles a T-square and hooks over the top of the canvas or, to avoid scraping the canvas in this case, he hooks it over two horizontal stretchers placed on top of the canvas. An adjustable block on the bottom of the guide keeps it a half-inch off the surface of the painting.
A. To the right of the canvas McLean has a "wipe-off paper" to remove excess paint from overloaded brushes, as well as to form fine points on the sable brushes. He ends up with all the gradations of, for example, skin tones, and can refer to the sheet as a color reminder. He has a drawer full of favorite wipe-off sheets, which have a beauty of their own.

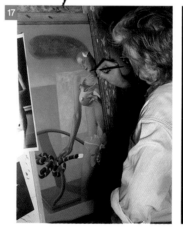

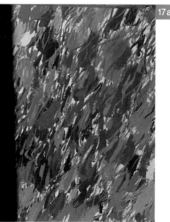

18

20

21

18 McLean's reference for the orchids, the snake head, and the black-and-white patterns he looked at for the tablecloth.

19 He begins to lay in the colors of the tablecloth on top of the texture put down in Step 3. Using an almost dry bristle brush he roughly paints in the blue-grey so the underpainting shows through. In the shadows he adds Cadmium Green Deep and Prussian Green in tiny amounts.

20 The green and yellow curving lines that link up to the bird shapes are more defined. The green is made with Turquoise mixed with Chinese Orange. The yellow is Cadmium Yellow Medium with White.
The bird shape is a creamy color of Flesh Tint with a touch of Orange, knocked back with quite a bit of White, keeping it pale. The stripe on the bird's body of brilliant Yellow Reddish is the last element to be added. In the shadow he darkens the stripe with a tiny bit of Crimson.

21 He paints the sky and clouds using Saturn Red, French Ultramarine Blue, Kings Blue Light, Flesh, Naples Yellow, and Cobalt Violet. The paint called "Flesh" is quite dark, almost an English Red, not pink.

22 The cloud shapes are becoming clarified, more color is built in, but he keeps it fairly rough; he doesn't want them finely finished, but "rather more impressionistic."

22

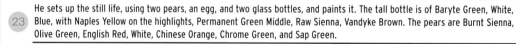

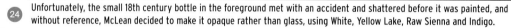

23. He sets up the still life, using two pears, an egg, and two glass bottles, and paints it. The tall bottle is of Baryte Green, White, Blue, with Naples Yellow on the highlights, Permanent Green Middle, Raw Sienna, Vandyke Brown. The pears are Burnt Sienna, Olive Green, English Red, White, Chinese Orange, Chrome Green, and Sap Green.

24. Unfortunately, the small 18th century bottle in the foreground met with an accident and shattered before it was painted, and without reference, McLean decided to make it opaque rather than glass, using White, Yellow Lake, Raw Sienna and Indigo.

25. Using the reference shown in Step 18, he completes the snake's head by adding Permanent Rose White and Kings Blue Light to the mix of Cadmium Yellow, Cadmium Yellow Deep, and Lemon Yellow Hue from Step 6. Yellow and Orange are added to the lower half of the head.

26. To complete the orchid, he moves inward from the white on the outside of the petals, gradually adding Naples Yellow, then Yellow Lake and Chinese Orange. The red stripes are Crimson, Ruby Lake, Permanent Red, and White with a dab of Yellow.

27. McLean felt the woman's closed mouth, the deep shadow emphasizing the crease from the nose, and even the arching curve of the eyebrows contributed to a hard quality he was not happy with. Using no reference, McLean repaints the entire face, starting by parting the lips to give her a softer feel. He lowers the eyebrows, softens the shadow areas and erases the crease. Her fuller cheekbones and highlighted, softened jawline make her face rounder and less angular. He changes her hairline and nose, and makes the ear recede. He lightens and adds pink to her skintones.
He had been apprehensive that by deciding to redo the head he was courting disaster. But as he looked at her hard features, he kept thinking "this won't do!" The changes make her vunerable, sweet, not simply beautiful and less hard. The changes, especially the decision to have the slightly prominant teeth, have given her a personality. To McLean, "she has been transformed into a much more appealing woman, not just this tough, good looking Amazon."

28. He tightens the hairline and adds texture, but uses the same colors from Step 2.
With meticulous care and attention to ongoing interelationships of color and form, the bird, flower and snake—the links from nature to the human—have been refined and sharpened throughout the development of the painting.

"Sphinx," Japanese calendar art

"Leopard," poster for Purina "Save the Big Cats"

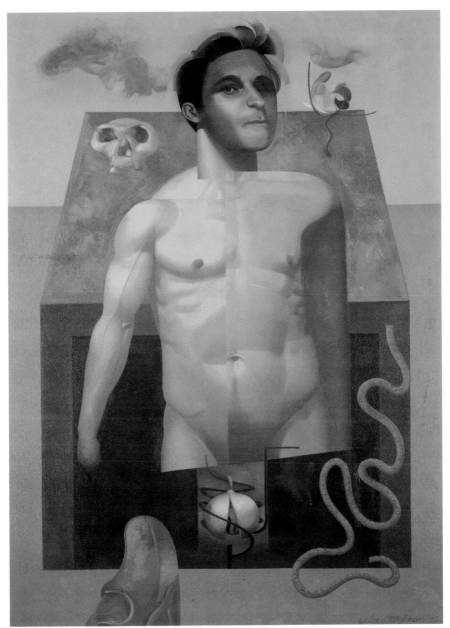

"Nude Male," rejected pharmaceutical illustration; Bill Shinn, Art Director

99
wilson
mclean

"Egg and Architecture," Geo Brief, supplement to <u>Chief Executive Magazine</u>; Alma Phipps, Art Director

"Detective with File Cabinet," <u>Playboy</u>; Kerig Pope, Art Director

"Fashion Spread, Men's Shirts," Playboy; Kerig Pope, Art Director

"Man in Scuptural Environment," for Lexmark; Pentagram, London

wilson
mclean

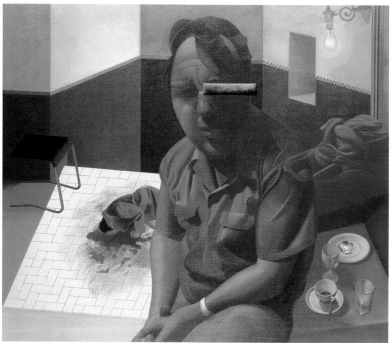

Born in Scotland, Wilson McLean moved to London at age ten. He attended art school at night while working on the staff of various magazines. After working as a free lance illustrator in Copenhagen and Spain, and for four years back in London, he moved to New York where he became established as a top illustrator. His awards include medals from the Art Directors Club of New York, and a "Clio" for a series of TV commercials. He has won eight Silver and four Gold Medals from the Society of Illustrators, as well as its Hamilton King Award for the best of show by a member. He received a Gold Medal from the Los Angeles Art Directors Club. McLean has had one-man shows at the Society of Illustrators, and in Savannah, Georgia. Two large exhibitions of his lithographs were held in Zurich. Included in many group shows nationwide, his work is held by the Smithsonian Institution and the Air and Space Museum in Washington, D.C., as well as in the London Transport Museum's Permanent Collection. To commemorate "European Music Year" in 1985, Great Britain commissioned McLean to design and illustrate five stamps for a special edition on British composers. He has taught and lectured throughout the U.S.

SIXTEEN YEARS AGO, WHEN NO
ONE ELSE IN THE ILLUSTRATION FIELD
WAS INTERESTED IN COMPUTERS,
BARBARA NESSIM, AN AWARD-WINNING
ILLUSTRATOR, TOOK IBM UP ON ITS
INVITATION TO EXPLORE ITS NEW,
EXTREMELY EXPENSIVE GRAPHICS
TECHNOLOGY—FOR FREE. NOW THE
GRANDE DAME OF THIS INCREASINGLY
POPULAR MEDIUM, SHE CREATES IMAGES
FOR PRINT—NOW ONLY FOR HIGH
PROFILE COMMISSIONS, GALLERY
SHOWS, AND FOR COMPUTERS THAT COM-
MUNICATE DIRECTLY WITH ONE ANOTHER.
SHE WORKS OUT OF AN ENORMOUS SOHO
LOFT THAT HAS ITS OWN GALLERY AREA,
AND IS FILLED BOOKS, PLANTS,
AND FLAT FILES OF WORKS DATING FROM
THE 1950S TO THE PRESENT. HER
COMPUTER STATION—WITH SHELVES OF
PROGRAMS AND MANUALS—IS LOCATED
BEHIND BOOKCASES THAT KEEP OUT THE
LIGHT FLOODING IN FROM A WALL OF
WINDOWS. HER DATABASE CONTAINS
400 IMAGES SCANNED FROM HER
SKETCHBOOKS WHICH SHE CAN
USE IN AN ENDLESS VARIETY OF
COMBINATIONS AND CONFIGURATIONS.
SHE CAN ALSO WORK AT HER OFFICE
AT PARSONS SCHOOL OF DESIGN WHERE SHE IS THE CHAIR OF THE
ILLUSTRATION DEPARTMENT—SHE NEED ONLY CARRY A DISKETTE
BETWEEN WORK STATIONS. A SERVICE PROVIDER WILL ENABLE HER
TO DOWNLOAD FROM ONE COMPUTER TO THE OTHER, BUT SHE
FEELS THE DISKETTE IS THE SAFEST WAY TO
TRANSFER HER WORK AT THIS TIME.

THE ASSIGNMENT:
although the original concept of
"Computer Love" had been intended
as a single image, computer-generated work,
once Nessim was given the assignment, it
quickly became a much more ambitious
project. She wanted to design an interactive,
**animated "Love" Web site. She
approached Janet Waegel, the Design
Director of Time Online, and they**
enthusiastically agreed it would
be an exciting project to explore—
with the possibility of eventually
getting online. During this project
her new Apple computer "crashed"
and she was not able to
access the animation, but we
were able to photograph the steps
at her Parsons station. Eventually,
Apple replaced the faulty system.
THE THOUGHT PROCESS: *nessim's
initial concept was of two figures
facing each other over a keyboard,
but after consideration, she decided
on a spider's web with hearts, making*

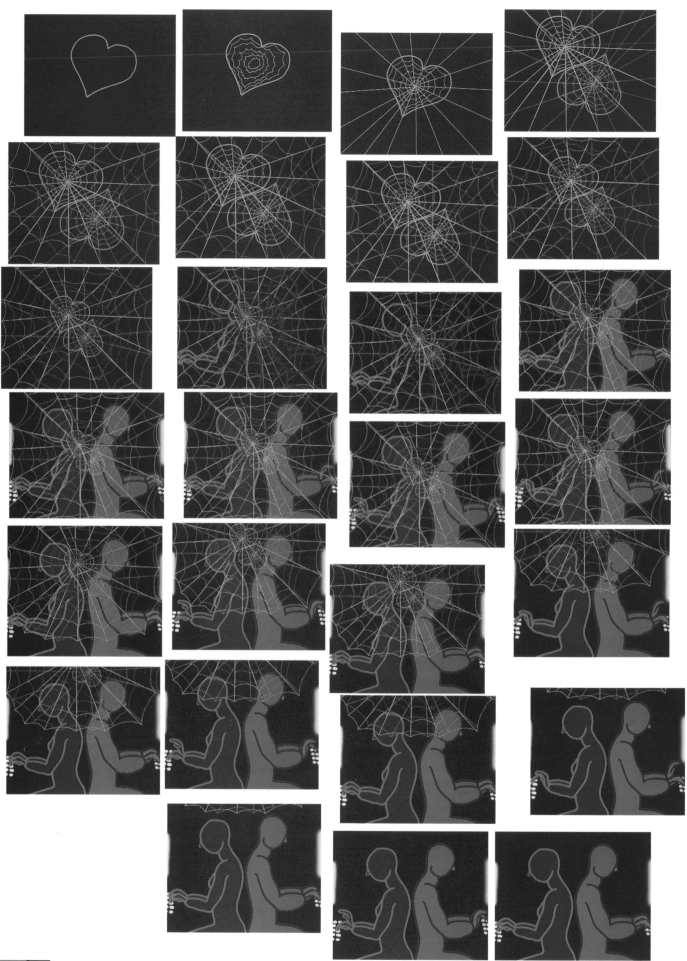

107

editorial[nessim

a visual pun of "love "on the web." at this early stage she anticipated the animation movement of the web—with hearts woven into it—moving up and revealing the couple beneath. she could envision this not only as a web site, but as a possible screen saver.

THE EQUIPMENT: 8500/120 16/IGIG/CD Apple computer. 2 x 32 MB DIMMs additional memory for the 8500. EA Research 30/1152 PCI video card Sony Multiscan Triniton 20 se monitor. 1X Extended Keyboard. AGFA Arcus II Scanner Laser Writer 16/600 pro printer. Syquest 88.
THE PROGRAMS: Photoshop, Macromedia Director 4.0

- -

Heather McGuire, Nessim's assistant, also a computer artist, worked with her throughout the project. She says "We had music going; it was like a little party. Even working on something technical, when there's more than one person, it's fun, and to see the animation come to life was exciting."

THE STEPS:

1 She found the figures of her initial sketch too specific; she wanted them to depict any race, religion, age, so she took a more generic approach.

2 The Love on the Web sketch: Even at this stage she thinks in computer colors, as noted on lower right. The final animation turned out, in this case, to be very close to her original ideas.

3 Nessim already has the animation movements in a rough layout by the time she meets with Design Director Janet Waegel to go over the concepts. Waegel says, "The transmissive nature of the screen itself allows color to glow intensely and beautifully." Because of Nessim's strong graphic line, Waegel could easily envision the imagery on the screen.

4 To fulfill the needs of this book Nessim decides to take the animation only to the point where the two figures are seated back to back, the web fully raised. Using the same techniques described here, Nessim and Waegel foresee the animation continuing into a close-up of the figures.

5 A rough layout from the end of existing animation through the close-up.

1a

1b

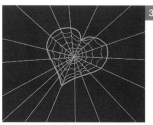

1c

ANIMATION STEPS

The following are the 29 screens created in Photoshop. Each screen is given a name: The first in this series is SIspWeb-01, which stands for Society of Illustrators Spider Web and the number of the screen. Using these images—some of which were repeated—the final 44-step animation was created with Macromedia Director with the technical assistance of Irina Sheynfeld, a programer for The Wall Street Journal Interactive Edition. The clock on the upper right reflects the fact that all the screens were shot by photographer Barcellona at one sitting. The actual creation of the animation took one weekend. The screen was set at 600 x 400 pixels and 72 DPI, standard for the Web— the images work on the monitor but prevent downloading clear images. Nessim notes that the larger the image, the slower the animation will perform.

A. Each element in the animation is put on layers. To create each layer, Nessim clicks on the default Layer Window. To begin, she chooses the Background option.

On the Color Picker Screen, Nessim decides on the background color. She chooses colors divisable by 51 for PC compatibility. She selects Mode on the menu bar, chooses Indexed Color and selects from the swatch window. The breakdown of the color appears on the screen: the HUE is 240, the SATURATION 100, and BRIGHTNESS 60. The percentages are 0 RED, 0 GREEN and 153 BLUE. The LIGHTNESS is 28, GREEN-RED AXIS is 62, and the BLUE-YELLOW AXIS is -75. CYAN is 96%, YELLOW 0%, MAGENTA 96% and BLACK 0%. (SIDEBAR 1) From this point on, she chooses the New Layer option for each element. After choosing colors and drawing figures, she names the layer. She manipulates layer placement in the Layer Window. They include: Background, Pink heart, Blue heart, Red figure, Blue figure, Web with hearts, Monitors and Keyboards.

B. She draws the pink heart (Sidebar 2) with the stylus on a Wacom tablet—she finds it easier than scanning in a drawing done on paper. She has used this method for sixteen years, even before they had tablets. "When you're doing an animation, there are some parts that need to be complicated, and some that must be simplified."

C. She uses the paintbrush option for most lines throughout the animation. She clicks on brush icon and chooses the diameter and hardness. While she works, she tries not to get too technical but uses all her artistic skills—line, color, composition—to create the images she wants. Her assistant, Heather McGuire, takes detailed notes throughout. Nessim also stresses the necessity to BACK UP everything as she goes along.

2 Inside the pink heart Nessim draws a web using the same color but a smaller brush.

3 Radiating lines come from the center of the heart. For this she uses the Straight Line tool.

4 Upside-down light-blue heart (Sidebar 3) has slightly darker radiating lines. The choice of color, Nessim says, was based on a "male/female, ying/yang kind of thing."

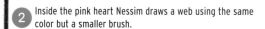

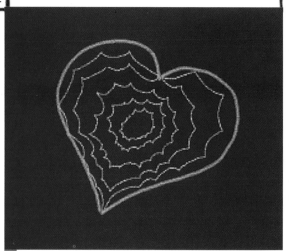

2

3

4

She continues to add to the webs. (5)

To darken the background color (Sidebar 4) she highlights the Background option in the Layer Window. In the tool box, she clicks on the Picker (the eyedrop icon), and makes a selection in the Swatch Window. Returning to the tool box she clicks on the Fill mode (spilled paint can icon). "As night turns to day, day turns to night;" she says, "this gives a sense of the passage of time." She also notes the deeper hue makes it easier to see the figures she will add later. "It's an aesthetic and meaningful choice." (6)

She continues to add more web as she begins to reduce the hearts. Selecting IMAGE on the menu bar, she chooses EFFECTS, then SCALE. To scale proportionally, she holds the Option and Shift keys down (a Constraint), she then continues to draw the web into the window space. (7)

More additions to the spider web, further reduction of heart shapes.   The process continues. (8) (9)

The hearts are reduced to their final size, the web expanded to its final size. (10)

Selecting a brush from the default BRUSH WINDOW, she draws the blue outline of the man (Sidebar 5) and red woman (Sidebar 6). Their layers appear in front of the web. (11)

A 12th screen was created, but discarded as unnecessary, so it was not brought into the Director folder for animation. (12)

She changes the position of the figure's layers in the LAYER WINDOW so they now appear behind the web. (13)

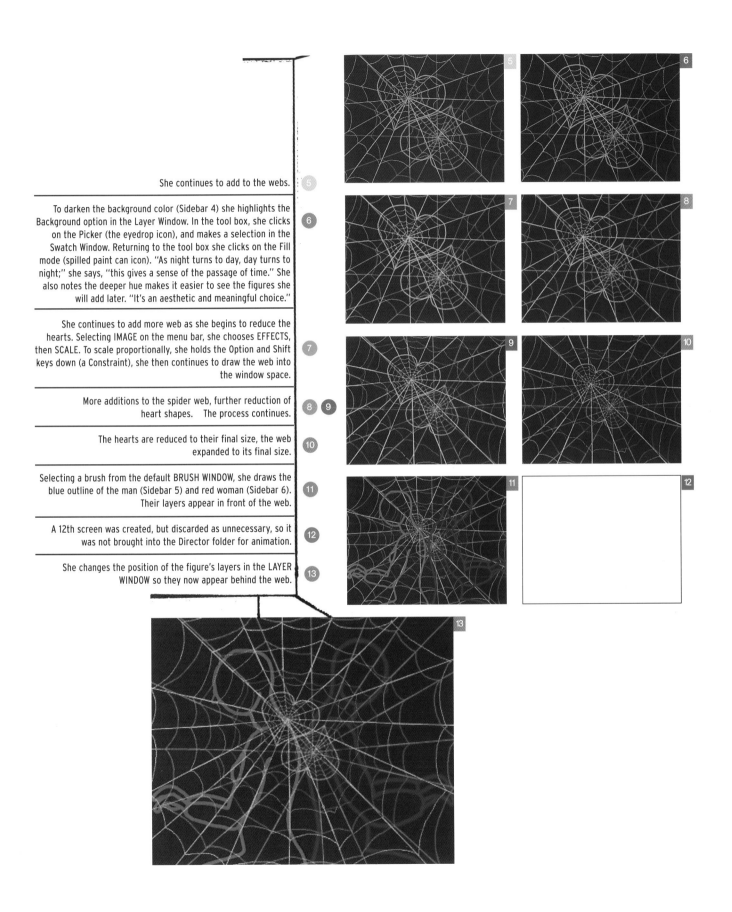

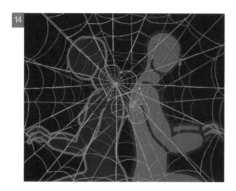

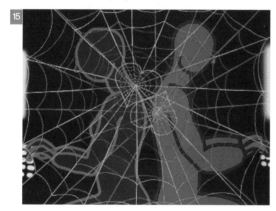

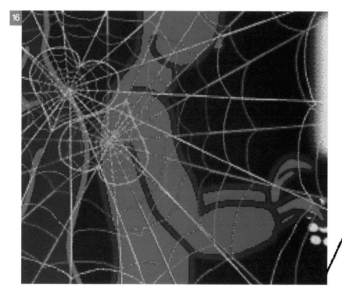

14 To fill in the man's figure, she first clicks on woman's body line to duplicate the color (Sidebar 6 see Step 11). Using the Fill mode she clicks on the man's body. At this point Nessim decides the color is too bright. She goes to the swatch window and takes it down three tones (Sidebar 7).

Through trial and error she decides to leave the man's hands and nose the bright red of the outside line (Sidebar 6). These elements are smaller and the hands will be animated, so she wants them to be more visible. As with traditional imagery—details are crucial, the subtle differences make the work believable—"they are the truth of the work."

She repeats the process of filling in the figure of the woman, the body (Sidebar 8) less bright than the man's outline (Sidebar 5), and the hands and nose brightened slightly (Sidebar 9).

15 She draws in the keyboards (Sidebar 10) with a regular brush and the monitors (Sidebar 11) using a Diffused Brush option. She wants to indicate them with the faintest glow and few details because "the monitor disappears when you're working on it—you're not aware of it."

16 She animates the man's left hand. She isolates the hand itself using the Lasso tool from the tool box. On the Menu bar, she selects Image, then Effects, then Rotate. Using the directional keys on her keyboard, she positions the hand exactly where she wants it. Then she redraws the part that had been hidden behind the right hand.

17 The woman's right hand goes up and the man's right hand goes up. Nessim wanted a snycopated motion, to give a more realistic action.

18 Woman raises left hand, man raises left hand.

19 Nessim raises the web layer to the level of their waists. Here she makes the edge of the web more scalloped by erasing the extraneous web lines from the layer, which adds to the curtain effect.

20 Web is at mid-arm, both their right hands are raised.

21 Web is at mid-arm, their hands are level.

22 Web to shoulders, left hands up.

23 Web to shoulders, hands level.

24 Web at mid-faces, right hands up.

25 Web at mid-faces, hands level.

26 Web above heads, left hands up.

27 Web above heads, hands level.

28 Web is gone, right hands up.

29 Web is gone, hands level.

30 Return to screen 1 of pink heart and the animation is complete.

31 Nessim at screen 31, McGuire taking notes.

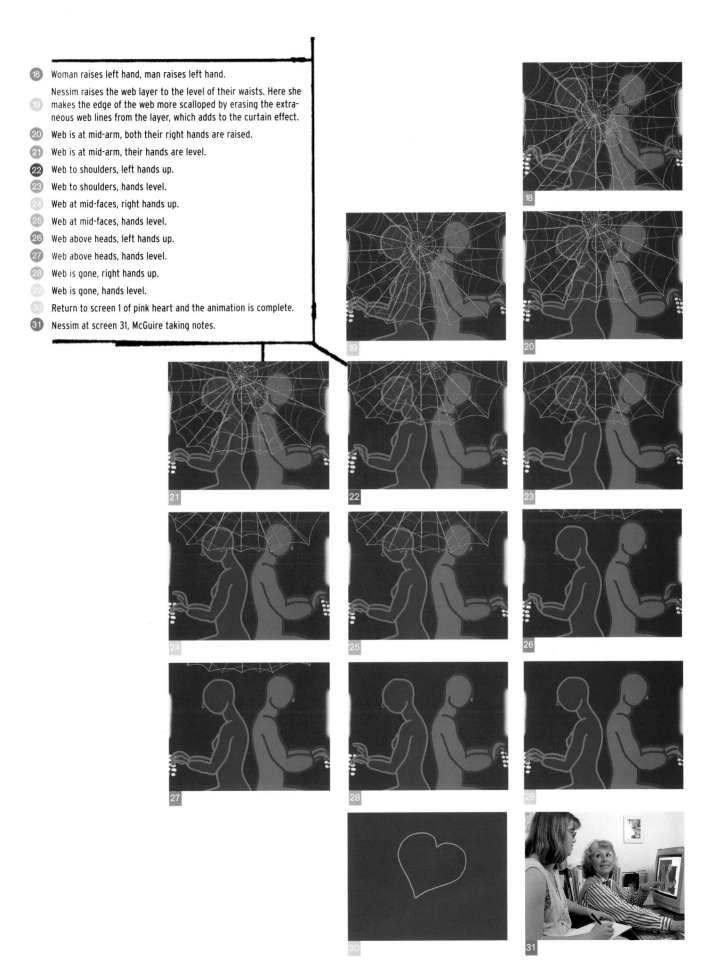

SIDEBAR 1 — BLUE BACKGROUND 1

H	240	L	28
S	100%	a	62
B	60%	b	-75
R	0	C	96%
G	0	M	96%
B	153	Y	0%
		K	0%

SIDEBAR 2 — PINK HEART & WEB

H	319%	L	72
S	60%	a	60
B	98%	b	-23
R	251	C	25%
G	101	M	62%
B	203	Y	0%
		K	1%

SIDEBAR 3 — LIGHT BLUE HEART & WEB

H	217%	L	73
S	68%	a	11
B	99%	b	-45
R	92	C	53%
G	154	M	36%
B	252	Y	0%
		K	1%

SIDEBAR 4 — BLUE BACKGROUND 2

H	240	L	12
S	100%	a	39
B	27%	b	-48
R	0	C	100%
G	0	M	100%
B	68	Y	29%
		K	10%

SIDEBAR 5 — BLUE OUTLINE OF MAN

H	240%	L	43
S	100%	a	83
B	100%	b	-98
R	0	C	87%
G	0	M	85%
B	255	Y	0%
		K	0%

SIDEBAR 6 — RED MAN NOSE, HANDS, OUTLINE OF WOMAN

H	0%	L	55
S	100%	a	76
B	100%	b	72
R	255	C	0%
G	0	M	91%
B	0	Y	100%
		K	0%

SIDEBAR 7 — RED MAN HEAD & BODY FILL

H	0%	L	47
S	100%	a	67
B	80%	b	63
R	204	C	11%
G	0	M	93%
B	0	Y	100%
		K	1%

SIDEBAR 8 — WOMAN BLUE FILL

H	240%	L	36
S	100%	a	73
B	80%	b	-89
R	0	C	92%
G	0	M	90%
B	204	Y	0%
		K	0%

SIDEBAR 9 — BLUE WOMAN HANDS & NOSE

H	240%	L	43
S	100%	a	83
B	99%	b	-99
R	0	C	87%
G	0	M	85%
B	254	Y	0%
		K	0%

SIDEBAR 10 — KEYBOARD

H	0%	L	
S	0%	a	
B	73%	b	
R	187	C	31%
G	187	M	20%
B	187	Y	20%
		K	2%

SIDEBAR 11 — COMPUTER SCREENS

H	181%	L	83
S	25%	a	-12
B	79%	b	-5
R	150	C	45%
G	200	M	4%
B	201	Y	121%
		K	1%

Throughout the creation of the screens in Photoshop, Nessim has been printing out black-and-white images of each screen, making duplicates of images that will repeat in the animation.

She makes a flip book—which was, of course, an early form of animation. Although this is not a necessary step, Nessim likes see how the whole thing hangs together.

At this point Irina Sheynfeld is called in as technical advisor to guide Nessim in the transfer from Photoshop to the Macromedia Director program to create the animation. With the proliferation of new graphics programs, Nessim is now on a "need-to-know" basis. Having learned many programs, she can easily learn new ones. Also, by attending computer conferences, she keeps current and can always find someone to guide her through the nuances of the newest programs, as well as upgrades of older ones.

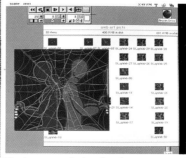

Director screen: Copies of each screen are made and renamed to include repeated images. Photoshop makes its own icons of each screen and when it's imported into Director, each one can be opened up. The directional keys at the top center manipulate the animation screens.

Nessim would deliver the animation job to the client on a Syquest 5.25 "Removable Cartridge."

Nessim has no patience with artists who say they don't like working on a computer before they've even tried it. Then, if they don't like it, fine—but she resents a close-minded attitude. She concedes that this is a time of exploration and because the roles are changing, sometimes one person ends up performing too many tasks and no one knows the parameters of their jobs. "Because computer illustrators or designers are asked to do so much, they can spend eighteen-hour days under great pressure instead of having time to think about what the best solution is—not necessarily the wildest and newest and weirdest one." However, with this medium, Nessim feels there are infinite possibilities and there will be options many illustrators don't imagine as yet, such as continuing use for their images rather than only for printed matter that is discarded.

"American Women: The Climb to Equality" Time Rudy Hoglund A.D., Irene Ramp Deputy A.D.

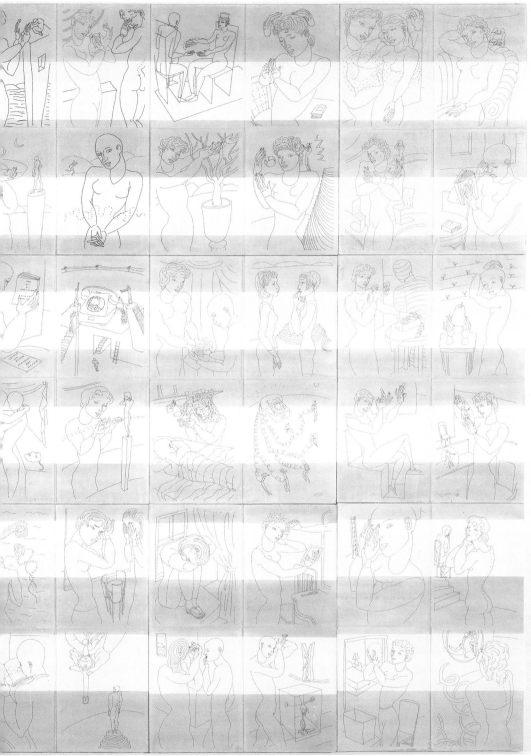

"America Lives" <u>P C Magazine</u> personal work-computer generated. Amiga computer, Polaroid output.

barbara nessim

top Rolling Stone, Fred Woodward, A.D., bottom "Levis Jeans for Woman," Levis/Foote, Cone & Belding, Keith Potter, A,D.

top left, "Picture Bride", Scenario, Andrew Kner, A.D.
center left, "Sex in America", New York magazine, Syndi Becker, A.D.
bottom left, "Childern in the Mirror", Boston Globe, Rena Sockolow, A.D.
right, personal work, sketchbook 65

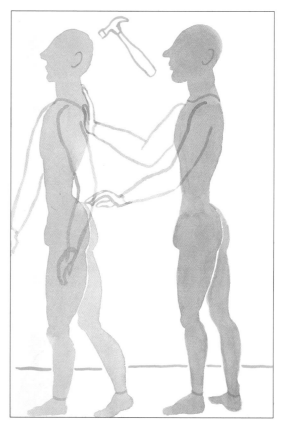

personal work, sketchbook 65

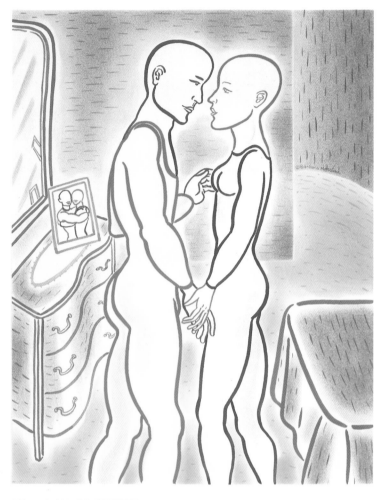

Born and raised in New York, Barbara Nessim studied at the High School of Art & Design and at Pratt Institute. Since 1963 her work has appeared in twenty one-person exhibitions in galleries and museums, including a series of computer generated shows titled "Random Access Memories 400" which appeared across American and in Bogota, Columbia. She has shown in well over a hundred group shows throughout the world and been featured or included in nearly forty books and countless articles published here and abroad. Her awards include Mac World's "Macintosh Masters Art Contest" Honors, 2nd International Digitart Competition, New American Talent '89/'90 from MoMA San Francisco, and over two hundred awards from trade organizations and publications since 1960. She has taught as artist-in-residence, lectured extensively, been a panelist and given seminars, juried and curated shows, and appeared on television. She has taught since 1977 and is currently Chairperson of the Illustration Department at Parsons School of Design. Her work is held in public and private collections.

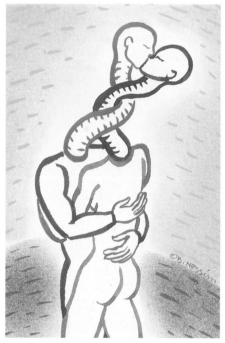

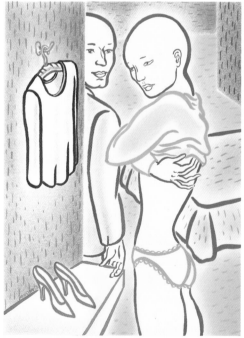

"Sex in America", Time
Arthur Hochstein, A.D.
Tom Miller, Designer

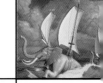

tim
o'brien

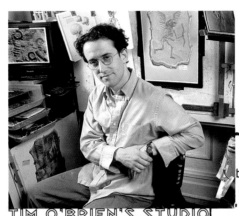

TIM O'BRIEN'S STUDIO
IS ON THE SECOND FLOOR
OF A CHARMING DUPLEX
IN A BROOKLYN BROWN-
STONE HE SHARES WITH HIS
WIFE, ELIZABETH PARISI, AN
ART DIRECTOR AT SCHOLASTIC.
THE SOMEWHAT CHAOTIC ROOM
WHERE THE 31-YEAR-OLD
ARTIST TURNS OUT NEARLY A
PAINTING A WEEK,
LOOKS OVER A LEAFY
BACKYARD AND A LARGE
FISH TANK FILLED WITH
HUGE, GOLDEN JAPANESE
FISH. BOOKCASES STUFFED
WITH ART AND REFERENCE
BOOKS, SHELVES PILED
WITH PAINTING SUPPLIES,
RACKS OF TAPES AND CDS
THREATEN TO ENCROACH ON
HIS WORK AREA. THE FORMER
BOXER IS KEPT COMPANY BY HIS
DOG, BUSKER, A TINY
FEATHERY-EARED PAPILLON.

THE ASSIGNMENT:
O'Brien, possessing a kind of
boyish innocence combined with
mature painterly skills, made a
good choice for the topic of
"First Love." Initially, the thought was to
have him depict a young couple in the
throes of their first romantic entangle-
ment. Known for his trompe l'oeil effects
and visual puns, it seemed O'Brien could
have some fun with this topic. After a
number of phone calls, it became clear
he was struggling to find something totally
unexpected and compelling. Interestingly,
because the assignment was for a book and
hence with some permanence, he viewed
it somewhat differently than for a
magazine illustration to be looked at once
and discarded. What he came up with was a
startling departure from the original concept,
but wonderfully creative.
For an actual editorial job, O'Brien, who prefers
tight deadlines, takes two days from phone call
to delivery. he faxes his preferred sketch,
enlarged from his sketchbook, plus an alter-
nate, "which often secures the one you want."
from mid-afternoon, when his sketch is o.k.'d
by the assigning art director and editor, until
eleven at night, he'll put reference material
together and shoot a polaroid. then he goes to
finish. he's never had to make a change in
an editorial piece. **THE THOUGHT PROCESS:**
his first sketch was of a chubby cupid coming through a love note with child's writing
on it—a ten year old's first love. he rejected
it as "stupid." adam and eve was
another theme. he also rejected an
image of a boy reading playboy,

FIRST CUPID
(CUPIDO PRIMUS)

THIS EARLY MESSENGER OF LOVE
WAS UNEARTHED IN PRISTINE CONDITION,
APRIL 18, 1908

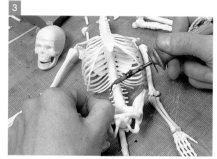

but, he says "i have to get the idea out of my head—it's like dust." he got stuck on the idea of a couple, each holding a cage over the other's head, first love being very focused and not allowing the rest of the world in. then he gave up for a month. finally, he had to "button down," and came up with the idea of an archaeological discovery of the first cupid.

REFERENCE:
He went to the Peabody Museum in Boston to look at fossils and found they were dark. By giving his first Cupid fossil a color also kept the image from looking like a dead baby, a morbid aspect he did not intend. He wasn't trying for complete accuracy—he's sure someone will note "that the iliac crest doesn't turn that way, the head isn't that size. I wanted to get the proportions close." For the baby's skull, he used the Atlas of Human Anatomy for the Artist by Stephen Rogers Peck, Oxford University Press. The Cupid reference came from his own library.

2 He makes the watercolor sketch on an Aquarelle Arches, 100% cotton, rough, 7-by 10-inch watercolor block. He uses block watercolors in a pan rather than tubes because they're more portable, though he's not fussy about the brand.

3 He sculpts the model from a Visible Man kit. Using reference, he scales it down, taking apart the bones in the spine to get the infantile curve of the neck. A heating element melts the plastic.

4 He modeled the skull from plasticine with sculpting tools, put the head on the body, then created wings out of plasticine—which he ended up changing later (see Step 9). He airbrushes the figure, using Burnt Umber. O'Brien always uses a respirator to protect his lungs.

1 O'Brien works on the initial sketch, surrounded by reference and discarded ideas. Because he wanted it to look like it was in a museum, he called a Latin professor for the correct term for First Cupid: Cupido Primos. He chose 1908 as the "date of discovery" because it sounded romantic, and April 18th in honor of his late father's birthday.

5 After constructing a foamcore box, he positions the Cupid and pours plaster around it, letting the skeleton sink in.

6 The model as O'Brien will photograph it with 160 Kodak tungsten film. He adjusts the lights to achieve the desired effect.

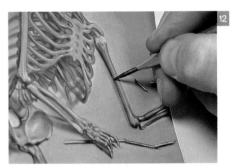

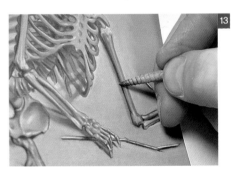

7 He uses double thick, hot pressed, Frisk illustration board. With a foam brush, he applies three or four very thin coats of grey gesso on the painting side letting each coat dry before applying the next. After the front dries, he applies two coats on the back of the board until the edges curl slightly forward, so when it's taped to the drawing board, which he constructed himself, it lies flat and doesn't "bounce" from the center.

8 After choosing the preferred image, he projects it onto the gessoed board then begins the drawing, using a 9H pencil and always using a paper shield to keep the oil from his hand off the surface. He prefers a Berol pencil because it has a darker tone than any other brand. For the whites he uses a General's White charcoal pencil. Blending stumps and kneaded erasers are used throughout the drawing process.

9 With the projected image on the side as reference, he puts values into the drawing. At this point, he discovers more realistic bird wings in a reference book. Deciding to be precise, he redraws them, and indicates the impression that wings with feathers would have made on the "tablet."

10 Blending the white pencil with a stump.

11 For texture, he picks pigment out of the white with an Eraser Stik.

12 Drawing into the arm with a 9H pencil.

13 Casting the shadow with a stump.

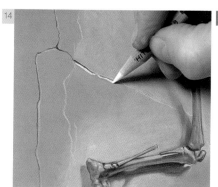

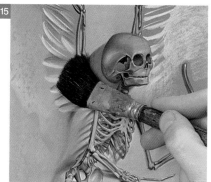

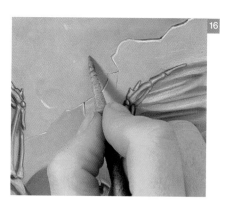

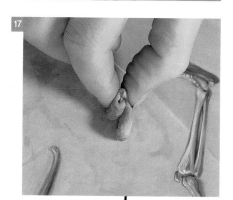

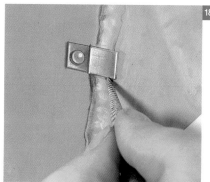

14 Making a "crack" with a white pencil. "The great thing about working on grey is that white represents light. When you work on white you create white by putting the darks in. When I paint, I also start from a neutral, middle ground and put in darks and whites."
He will use the same techniques throughout the drawing.

15 He softens the impression of wings with a stiff dry brush. This is a shortcut for blending large areas—rather than using the stump.

16 By knocking down the value using the stump, he shifts the tablet back slightly where it is cracked.

17 To make the tablet realistic and interesting, he draws random shapes throughout in white pencil. Here he makes other forms by rolling around a strangely-shaped kneaded eraser to create irregularity.

18 The brackets he renders from memory, without reference.

19 Referring to a book on paleontology, he renders the fossil impression on the lower right-hand side. An electric eraser makes a crisp line into the white.

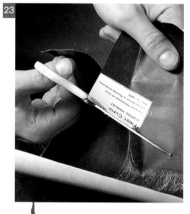

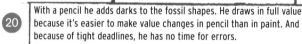

20. With a pencil he adds darks to the fossil shapes. He draws in full value because it's easier to make value changes in pencil than in paint. And because of tight deadlines, he has no time for errors.

21. The finished drawing. The long crack in the lower portion of the tablet points to where the label will be positioned. It's a design element which will pull the label into the overall picture plane.

22. Because he doesn't want to cut into his illustrations using traditional frisket, O'Brien has devised a method for masking areas not to be painted: He makes a photocopy of the drawing, in sections if necessary. Instead of Xerox paper, the copy is made on 8 1/2-by-11-inch Matte Adhesive Film for Plain Paper Copiers by Tekra. It is semi-transparent and has a light adhesive on the back. He cuts out the tablet shape from the Tekra mask, saving the border for later use. He peels off the backing and, without burnishing, tacks it down onto the drawing.

23. The label is a custom-made "rubdown" transfer of text reproduced onto adhesive film. He created text on a Macintosh and sent it to Graphic Lab. He makes a copy of the rubdown on the Matte Adhesive Film. Here he cuts out a label-shaped mask.

24. With a Paasche airbrush he paints the label area white.

25. After the white dries, he puts down the rubdown mask. Then he airbrushes the background in beige, a value darker than the white label.

26. Peeling off mask on tablet area and label.

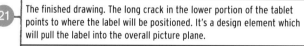

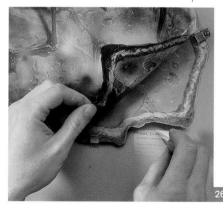

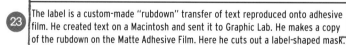

editorial o'brien

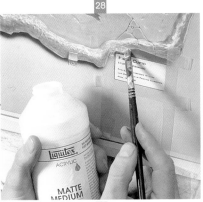

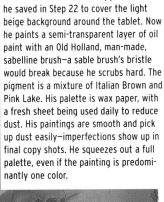

27 He has applied spray fixative to the drawing before putting the real rubdown with a burnishing tool. Otherwise, spray fixative would melt the rubdown.

28 After he has put a mask of Scotch Magic Tape around the edge of the label, he paints on Liquitex Matte Medium to protect it from the pigment.

29 He's used the border of copy mask which he saved in Step 22 to cover the light beige background around the tablet. Now he paints a semi-transparent layer of oil paint with an Old Holland, man-made, sabelline brush—a sable brush's bristle would break because he scrubs hard. The pigment is a mixture of Italian Brown and Pink Lake. His palette is wax paper, with a fresh sheet being used daily to reduce dust. His paintings are smooth and pick up dust easily—imperfections show up in final copy shots. He squeezes out a full palette, even if the painting is predominantly one color.

30 He adds lights to the medium value of the tablet to bring up the skeleton. To create an illusion of depth, he puts white next to a shadow or a dark edge to make it pop out.

31 To make divots and air pockets in the tablet, he uses Burnt Umber and a sable brush—the brush he uses for all rendering. The yellow slashes of paint and blue dots are done in the same random manner as in the drawing, shown in Step 17. These are the "happy mistakes."

32 Subtle value differences are made by putting thicker paint in dark areas.

30

31

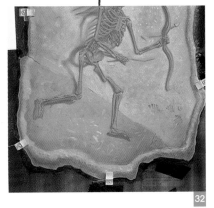

32

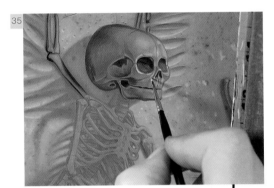

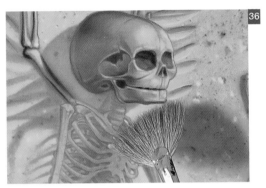

33 He spatters with a bristle brush to achieve texture, using Burnt Umber with a little Violet.

34 Painting in the bones with a fine sable brush and Burnt Umber.

35 Putting in lights. The principle throughout the painting is to widen the medium value pattern laid down in Step 29 by darkening the darks and lightening the lights.

36 He blends out the dappled brush strokes, section by section, with a fan brush; they are not blurry, but neither are they hard-edged. He doesn't use the fan brush to change values, only to create a gradation and to soften. The value changes must be painted in with a sable brush, otherwise the painting will "look like wax."
At this point, O'Brien decides to make a change. After looking at the whole painting, he discovers he wants to give a more chiseled and chipped-out appearance to the tablet so it doesn't look man-made.

Using the same technique throughout, he completes the illustration. He glazes down shadows behind the Cupid's head using a transparent Magenta, so the object on the tablet is a different color than the tablet. The brackets get a touch of blue and a highlight, and a drop shadow is painted in to secure the tablet against the "wall." "The Cupid works on many levels. First love–the very first Cupid–the archeological pun. But it also indicates the crushing loss of first love. That changes the way you feel and love is never again the same. Not in a negative way, but the fear that you may be alone again is always present."

To deliver the job, he constructs a foamcore box, keeping a space between the lid and the painting. He posts "Wet Painting" warnings so those who open it don't touch the surface. His representative will deliver the illustration to the client.

"Slam," Scholastic Books, Elizabeth Parisi, A.D.

129

tim
o'brien

Untitled

tim
o'brien

top left Time, Arthur Hochstein, A.D, top right Time, Arthur Hochstein, Ken Smith, A.D.s, bottom Time, Arthur Hochstein, Jane Frey, A.D.s

tim
o'brien

top The Atlantic Monthly, Mary Workman, A.D, bottom Untitled

Untitled

top Untitled, bottom "Blade to the Heat," Mark Taper Forum, Chris Komuro, A.D.

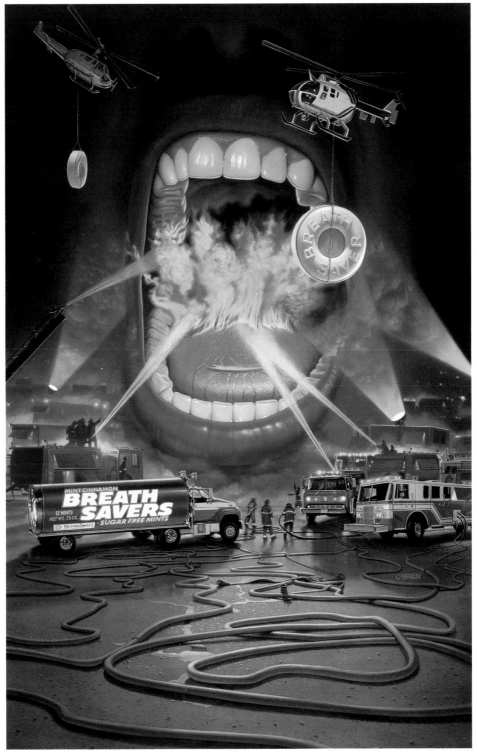

Untitled

tim
o'brien

Entertainment Weekly, Florian Bachleda, A.D.

Time, Arthur Hochstein, Ken Smith, A.D.s

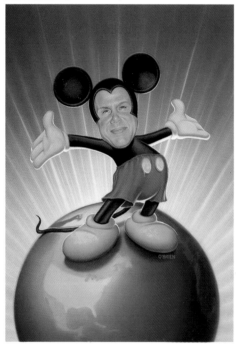

Raised in North Haven, Connecticut, Tim O'Brien studied with Rudolf Zallinger, Ken Davies, Leonard Everett Fischer, Howard Munce, Dennis Luzak and others at Paier College of Art. His first editorial job was for Playboy magazine and now his work appears there and in Time, Newsweek, New York, Entertainment Weekly, Atlantic Monthly, Forbes, Premier, and Mad. He has also illustrated hundreds of book jackets and has had many advertising clients. First noticed by the Society of Illustrators as a student when he was included in their Student Scholarship Competition, he has been regularly included in their annual exhibitions in the last ten years. He is also a teacher and trains heavyweight boxers in the sport he practiced before turning to illustration.

SURROUNDED ON TWO SIDES BY HIS COLLECTION OF DOLLS AND MASKS, MEL ODOM WORKS IN A SMALL STUDIO IN HIS WEST SIDE APARTMENT. ONE CABINET IS FILLED WITH BARBIE DOLLS, ANOTHER WITH HIS OWN CREATION, "GENE MARSHALL," A NATIONALLY MARKETED '40S STYLE DOLL WITH A SOPHISTICATED, HOLLYWOOD WARDROBE. ON THE WALL OVER HIS WORKTABLE, PICTURES OF GENE TIERNEY, ONE OF HIS IDOLS, ARE PART OF AN ECLECTIC COLLAGE THAT INCLUDES POLAROIDS OF THE TV SCREEN, PHOTOS OF PAST AND PRE-SENT GLAMOUR GIRLS AND THE BOXER EVANDER HOLYFIELD.

THE ASSIGNMENT: *odom's dangerously* sensual line and the sexy subject matter he often depicts in his illustrations made him a natural to depict the erotic aspect of love. He understood the market would be general, so certain constraints as to content would apply. We discussed his sketches and then, just as on an actual job, after approval he went to finish. In general, he doesn't show color sketches, but will discuss any restrictions the client might have.

THE THOUGHT PROCESS: Odom enjoyed the relative freedom of the assignment, though he thought of it as a real editorial assignment for a magazine—to keep it abstract, but erotic, was the challenge. At first he intended to do a finish of a *sketch that showed the man's face in full. however, as he studied the other two sketches, he discovered that the aspect of blindness depicted in one of them took on an importance for him. "in love," he said, "you're not seeing, you're acting." also, the sketch worked best on a visual level. he liked the way one light area inside the dark area made one fairly phallic shape on the middle of the page.   though not readily apparent, because of its position the white*

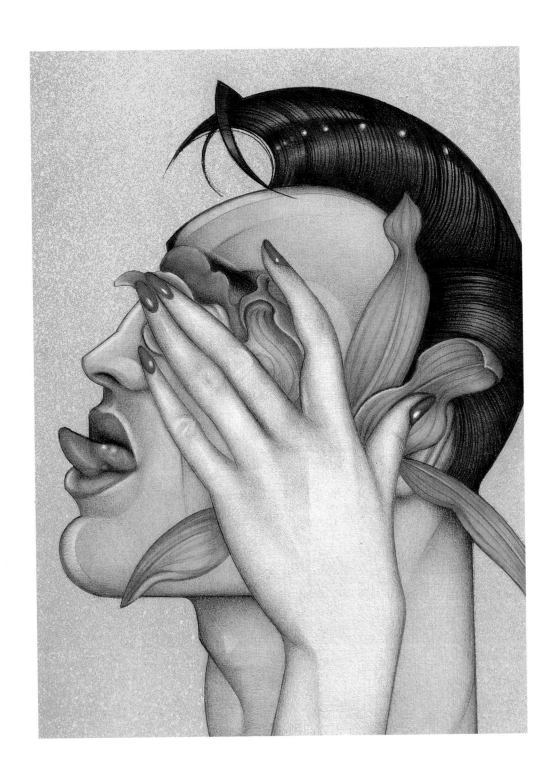

hand could be seen as the man's own. for odom, this is a subtle, unconscious reaction: "i don't think of these things until i've looked at the sketches a long, long time. then, i begin to realize the under-pinnings of my logic." he likes a visual that is open to interpretation or a subcon-scious thought that he's not privy to during the act of drawing. that is why he operates on the visual level alone when he draws, usu-ally with the tv or the radio on. to him, what will look best is the important thing. not intellectualizing keeps the images fresher and as beautiful as possible.

RESEARCH: Odom refers to an orchid book that he has used frequently. As one of his favorite images, Odom understands how this flower alone creates an erotic symbol for the viewer. The man's face is a photo of a gay porn model he's used many times, a man with a broken nose that's beautiful to draw. For him, the pornogra-phy reference gives him faces that are not com-posed, but are of people going through extremes. He also used a photo of Norma Schearer by Cecil Beaton, wanting to capture the tilt of her head. He says, "Everything on earth is potential refer-ence—even Polaroids off the television. For an illustrator, reference is money in the bank and useful for years."

THE STEPS:

1 Creating the initial sketches: Using a French Curve template, he draws the man's full face onto translucent vellum paper with Venus pencils ranging from H to 6B. At this stage he removes lines with a pencil eraser for convenience, rather than looking for the kneaded eraser. He uses templates to reenforce and make definite his more continued lines—though he can do it by hand, the templates make them perfect each time. Sometimes he must repeat an identical line three or four times; the template keeps it perfect.

2 Using the orchid reference, he draws the flower in the woman's hand. He tries to be realistic, because to him orchids are "astonishing combinations of colors—Mother Nature, God or Buddha did such a good job, who am I to change it? An orchid looks to be at a very precarious point between looking like an animal and a plant."

3 Having sketched the hand and head separately, he can manipu-late them to his liking—even reversing them. Sometimes, at this stage, accidents will affect what he draws. He believes it's important to remain open—it maintains playfulness and spon-taneity. He then traces the image onto another piece of vellum. Here he bends the vellum back to show its transparency.

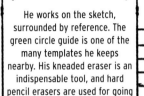

He works on the sketch, surrounded by reference. The green circle guide is one of the many templates he keeps nearby. His kneaded eraser is an indispensable tool, and hard pencil erasers are used for going into small areas.

With lines, he indicates the man's hair, giving it form. On the sketch he keeps the lines light, for they may be erased or changed.

The three completed sketches. After consideration, he chooses the center sketch, where the two figures become one, as described above.

He can envision this image on a huge scale, which signals its graphic strength. He likes how the fingertips, petals, tongue, and even the man's nose, have a shared, plant-like outward movement.

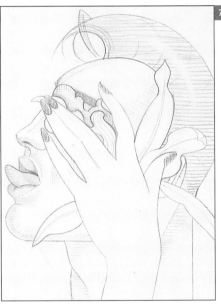

He has a same-size Xerox made of the sketch. He likes to keep his vellum sketches, to reuse elements from them or to give as gifts.

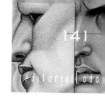

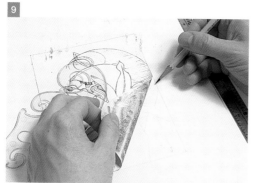

9 Using a 6B pencil, he has covered the back of the Xerox, making a transfer. He lifts the Xerox to check how the transfer is going onto a 10-by 13-inch Strathmore 100% rag illustration board. This surface readily absorbs the Peerless Dyes Odom uses.

10 Having gone over the entire drawing in pencil to reenforce the line—the template is very important at this stage—he paints maskoid over the hand, using Winsor & Newton water-colour Art Masking Fluid and an old brush. This keeps the hand white. He also lays down maskoid on the highlights of the hair, tongue, and fingertips. He cleans the brush in water.

11 Odom has found that Peerless Dyes do not fade, as do other dyes he's tried, and they come in "gorgeous colors." He paints a flesh color—a Burnt Sienna with some Yellow-Orange—over the entire surface. A large, round Grumbacher bristle brush helps blend the edges of the wash of flat tone.

12 With a small sable watercolor brush, he paints in the orchid color, a mix of Peerless Dye Violet and a small amount of Crimson. He uses tiny tips of bristles for detail work.

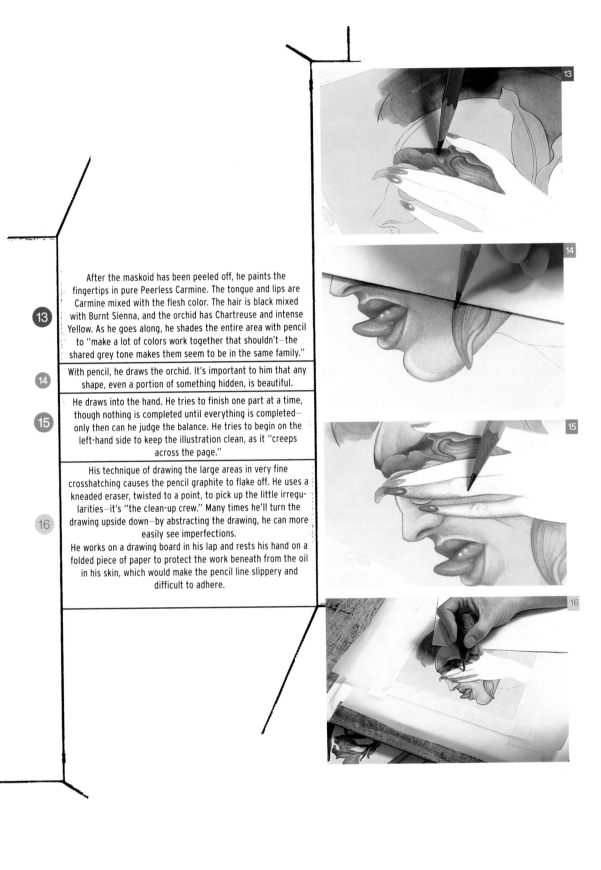

13 After the maskoid has been peeled off, he paints the fingertips in pure Peerless Carmine. The tongue and lips are Carmine mixed with the flesh color. The hair is black mixed with Burnt Sienna, and the orchid has Chartreuse and intense Yellow. As he goes along, he shades the entire area with pencil to "make a lot of colors work together that shouldn't—the shared grey tone makes them seem to be in the same family."

14 With pencil, he draws the orchid. It's important to him that any shape, even a portion of something hidden, is beautiful.

15 He draws into the hand. He tries to finish one part at a time, though nothing is completed until everything is completed—only then can he judge the balance. He tries to begin on the left-hand side to keep the illustration clean, as it "creeps across the page."

16 His technique of drawing the large areas in very fine crosshatching causes the pencil graphite to flake off. He uses a kneaded eraser, twisted to a point, to pick up the little irregularities—it's "the clean-up crew." Many times he'll turn the drawing upside down—by abstracting the drawing, he can more easily see imperfections.
He works on a drawing board in his lap and rests his hand on a folded piece of paper to protect the work beneath from the oil in his skin, which would make the pencil line slippery and difficult to adhere.

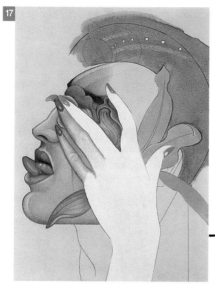

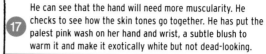

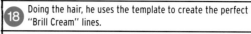

17 He can see that the hand will need more muscularity. He checks to see how the skin tones go together. He has put the palest pink wash on her hand and wrist, a subtle blush to warm it and make it exotically white but not dead-looking.

18 Doing the hair, he uses the template to create the perfect "Brill Cream" lines.

19 At this point, Odom feels he is almost "home," having completed the more difficult central area, confident about continuing the hair, petals, neck and part of the ear. It has taken him nearly ten hours to complete Steps 17 to 19. "But it looks just like I want it to look. You owe it to yourself to do it precisely the way you want."

20 The drawing is complete. The watercolor dye washes can be "sloppy"—outside the lines—because the background will be painted with gouache, which is opaque and will cover the rough edges. This is the point at which any preconceived thoughts about background color come to an end. All the colors in the drawing will change by adding a color to this large area. "It's the one part that's a crapshoot. Sometimes I do know, but frequently it doesn't work and I must try four or five changes in color."

To complete the background, he can have no distractions—no one in the studio, no music, no TV. For Odom it's the most instinctive use of color and the most vague; he wants no influences on him.

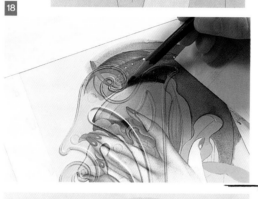

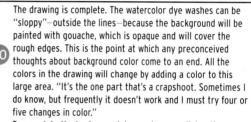

21 He paints the background using Winsor & Newton gouaches with sable brushes of various sizes.
He adds grey with every color he uses in the background because of the pencil tone. Otherwise, the brightness of the gouaches would overwhelm the tone of the drawing.
He chooses Chartreuse as the first color, echoing the color in the orchid at the center of the image. One of his favorite colors, "It goes beautifully with flesh. It is the color of newest growth; I like the fresh, slightly acidic quality—the color of Spring."
He says it pays to stick with one brand of gouache. For the background he used Winsor & Newton colors which he keeps in a cigar box: Naples Yellow, Permanent White, Chartreuse, Lamp Black, Charthamus Pink, Cadmium Orange, Golden Yellow.
The highlights on the hair, fingers, and tongue are white paper. Masking them out gives a softer effect than painting them on.

22 Before painting in the background, when the lines were still sharp, he had traced the drawing onto frosted acetate #003. Then with an X-Acto blade, he had cut a stencil. Whenever the stencils are really beautiful, he saves them.
He weights the stencil down with pennies and paper clips. With his thumb, he spatters colors onto the background using a variety of toothbrushes he has for this purpose—from soft to stiff.
Surrounded by saucers full of paint, he does the spatter work on the floor. Because he can't see the image under the stencil, he lets it dry, lifts the stencil and looks at it, sometimes for a long time before he realizes it's finished.

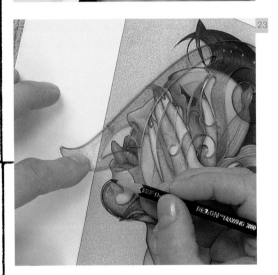

23 He redraws the edges. Again, the template is necessary. Seeing the perfect edges again, he can determine if the color is right. He then takes it into another room to view it in a different atmosphere, and will even take it to a coffee shop for a fresh look.
When Odom redraws the lines around the border, it is a declaration that he has finished and has once again held to his philosophical beliefs. "Shortcuts do not work. What's the point if you're cheating yourself?" He'd rather go to another medium than change his method, with all its personal quirks and difficulties. By using a man's head, a woman's hand, an orchid, and a tongue, he felt that many aspects of sexuality could be implied.
Finally, he covers the original with clear acetate, takes it personally or FedExes it to the client.

144

"Mother's Day," an illustration for a short story in Playboy.

Tornado Alley, by Craig Nova, Dell Publishing

In the Country of Desire, by Leslie Garrett, HarperCollins

The Magus, by John Fowles, Dell Publishing

Why We Never Danced the Charleston, by Harlen Green, Penguin Books

original portrait of Gene Marshall

Merab's Beauty, Harper & Row

Logo for "Three," a paper company

Mel Odom holds a BA in illustration from Virgina Commonwealth
University. Since 1975 he has been working as an illustrator in New
York for such clients as The New York Times Magazine, GQ,
Interview, Rolling Stone and has regularly contributed to Playboy
since 1979. He has created covers for Time, Das Magazine, Blueboy,
the Pennsylvania Gazette, Post Graduate Medicine, the Manhattan
Catalogue, Barbie Bazaar, and Omni magazine. His illustrations have
graced the covers of many books, including works by Anne Rice,
Ruth Rendell, Craig Nova, Edmund White, Augstin Gomez Arcos, and
Leslie Garrett. He has received many awards from the Society of
Illustrators and other arts organizations. Two books of his drawings
have been published: First Eyes, and Dreamer; and his first fashion
doll, Gene Marshall, has been launched nationwide.

Congratulations! You're ready to enter the professional world of illustration. Techniques sharp, you're as comfortable smudging charcoal on newsprint as you are inching a trackball across a Quark file. Your home page is up and humming, and your new portfolio is organized and professionally mounted. You're ready for your first assignment. So why doesn't the phone ring? Even more scary, what do you say when it does?

"Hello, is this Tina Newart?" a voice on the phone says. "I'm the director of the Society of Organic Asparagus Planters. We at SOAP like that Belgian endive you put on your web page. I need a pink asparagus, and I'm considering you and a number of other artists for the job."

"Cool," you're thinking, "my first real job."

"We're not-for-profit and we have no art budget," he continues, "but you'll get great exposure on the cover of our Magazine of Organic Asparagus. It reaches lots of influential people."

"Hmm," you scratch your head, "it sounds like it could be a good deal." You get hit with a shaft of brilliance. "Will I get credit?" you ask.

"Sure, sure," he says, "whenever someone calls to ask about the cover art, we'll tell them it was you." Then, as an aside, he says, "I'll fax over a purchase order. Fax it right back with your signature. It's just a formality, but our legal department insists on it."

Squinting at the faded grey type you see the words, "this work shall be considered a `work made for hire,' authorship and all rights are transferred to the commissioning agent." You call the client back and ask what this means. You discover that this organization runs the world's largest trade show on organic gardening, and they want to use your cover art as the logo. Even more, they intend selling thousands of T-shirts, aprons and tote bags with your art on them. "Listen," he says, "there are lots of other illustrators out there who'd jump at this opportunity. Take it or leave it."

Do you take the deal? Do you walk away? Do you negotiate a compromise? Maybe you were one of the smarter ones in school who didn't cut that special class on contracts and copyright. A little more street-wise, you joined the Graphic Artists Guild as a student, and got the same benefits as the pros at half the cost. Better prepared than most of the others entering the market, you know your first client will be an executive looking for the most he can get at the lowest rate. You know he isn't a designer or an artist, he doesn't know Helvetica from Boldoni, or scratchboard from gouache—and he cares even less. Okay, so you missed the negotiation class because you were on deadline for your term project. What do you do now?

You need to organize. Join the union that represents your craft and trade—the Graphic Artists Guild. It's the best way for you to turn situations like these to your advantage. The Guild's mission is to promote and protect the economic interests of member artists. It is committed to improving conditions for all creators of graphic arts and raising the standards for the entire industry. The Guild embraces all creators of graphic arts intended for presentation as originals or reproductions at all levels of skill and expertise.

Student membership in the Guild is valid for one year beyond graduation. It's the Guild's way of helping you get on your feet. Taking advantage of Guild programs and networking opportunities will equip you with the skills you need to compete more effectively in the market, and get the best deals you can. You'll have access to the artist-to-artist hotline, the latest industry news, and the opportunity to network and learn from seasoned pros who are helpful and generous. Every good deal you make helps not only you, but the entire industry. Every bad deal you make drags the whole industry with you. Good deals come with knowledge and experience. The Guild will give you both.

Paul Basista
Executive Director Graphic Artists Guild

Acrylics: Water soluble paints based on emulsion polymer acrylics thinned with water. They dry quickly, are very flexible and can be applied in thick layers. Suitable on canvas and other supports, they retain impasto and textural effects. Known for the brilliance of their color, they can imitate a variety of technical effects.

Airbrush: A technique in which pigments are applied as a controlled spray using compressed air or carbon dioxide. Subtle gradations of tone and finely blended colors can be produced by overlaying thin mists of paint. Combined with stencils or masks, they can produce hard- or soft-edged patterns.

Blending or drawing stump: Grey paper rolled to a point on one or both ends with which to rub pencil, colored pencil or pastel into gradations of tone.

Brayer: A small hand roller used to spread ink thinly and evenly over printing surfaces including plates, lithography stones, wood block, etc.

Brushes: Used for the application of paint, though also suitable for drawing with inks. Available in a large variety of shapes and sizes, they are made from different types of animal hair as well as synthetically.
  Bristle: Most important hard-hair brush, made from back of a pig, carries paint well. Range up to 12 sizes.
  Sable: Best soft hair, from the tail of the sable marten, known for strength and flexibility. Range up to 17 sizes.
  Synthetic: Inexpensive, but lack quality. Best used with acrylics which require water clean up.
  Rounds (Pointed): Round brushes that come to a point, ideal for small detail.
  Rounds (Blunt-ended): Round brushes that end in a dome shape and are used for large paint loads for wet-in-wet work.
  Brights: Rectangular shape with short hair, carry a load of paint, and can delineate sharp corners.
  Flats: Shallow, oblong brush ending in a straight edge, make angular marks, or long, broad strokes.
  Filberts: Shallow, oblong brush ending with a rounded tip offering possibilities of a flat and a round.
  Fan shaped: Used only to blend, have a thin, flat head with hair spread in a semi-circle.

Canvas: A textile support for any type of paint.
  Linen: A strong, finely woven, grey-brown cloth of medium weight available in fine and extra-fine.
  Cotton duck: Less expensive and readily available. A middleweight, soft, more open weave than linen. Both materials are available in a prepared state either stretched or in lengths with an acrylic ground not necessarily appropriate for all techniques.

Charcoal: Partially burned wood that is converted to carbon. Available in shape of original wood, as compressed charcoal, and as pencils with charcoal leads. Used primarily for sketches and preliminary drawings on painting support, though can be finished work.

Chinese ink: High quality black ink in stick form that when diluted, can produce an infinite variety of greys.

Collage: An image created by using pre-existing images or scraps of various materials glued to a support.

Colored pencils: Crayon-like leads encased in wood that can be sharpened to a fine point, made by a variety of manufacturers.

Copy shot: Reproduction-quality photograph of artwork taken under color-balanced lighting for true representation of the image.

Crosshatching: Two sets of parallel strokes placed one over the other in approximately opposite directions to cover the paper or ground.

Drying oils: Vegetable oils used in painting which combine with oxygen to produce a solid film resistant to the atmosphere and many solvents.
  Linseed oil: Most durable and thorough drying of natural oils.
  Stand oil: Made from alkali-refined linseed oil, possessing improved qualities. It makes paint flow and gives an enamel-like finish without showing brushstrokes. Ages well and yellows little.

Dye marker: A large variety of markers from many manufacturers provide drawing implements in many widths and colors. They are available with water-soluble inks, permanent inks, reflective inks such as Day-Glo, and metallic inks in gold, silver and copper.

Easels: A stand on which to hold a canvas or panel while painting. Studio easels are wood and well constructed in an A shape to hold heavy works. May feature castors, screw operated raising devices to adjust level, attached paint box or brush tray. Compact table easels can be convenient for smaller areas or traveling.

Fixative: Packaged in spray cans or bottles in matte, workable, clear finishes, they stabilize the drawing surface and offer a degree of protection for pencil, charcoal, colored pencils, and pastels.

French curve: A template available in a variety of shapes including hyperboles, parabolas, and ellipses.

Frisket: Produced in sheets or rolls, frisket has a light adhesive and is used for masking areas for painting, airbrush, and stippling.

Gesso: A white, absorbent ground containing chalk or clay. Although a gesso ground can be mixed in the studio, commercial products are readily available.

Glazing: Primarily used in oil painting, glazing is the use of transparent layers of color which allow the image beneath to remain visible. When used in other media it is more correctly called a "wash."

Gouache: An opaque watercolor which can be bound with gum, though waterbased paints can be rendered opaque by the addition of white. Popular for its speed of use, its flat, contrasting colors are easily reproduced.

Ground: A base layer that acts as a buffer between the support and the painting, and gives the support a more suitable surface on which to paint.

Illustration board: A smooth-surfaced, thin board made from pasted up sheets of paper. Bristol board is a standard, quality board available in a variety of surface textures (see Paper) and thicknesses, called plys.

Liquid masking solutions: A liquid rubber which may contain a coloring ingredient to make it more visible. Good for masking large areas or high-lights. Removed by rubber cement pick-up or by rolling off with fingers.

Masking: To deliberately shield an area when painting, so that when the masking is removed, the area beneath it remains untouched. Also, it can be used to protect finished areas of a painting while surrounding sections are worked upon. Low tack masking films are available for airbrush use.

Medium: An ingredient, such as oil or gum, mixed with pigment to form paint. The term also refers to mixtures added to paint in order to modify its handling properties and finish.

Oil paints: High quality pigments directly mixed with a refined drying oil, a blend of drying oils, or thickened drying oils. Prepared to a thick consistency, yet not stiff, they are rich in pigment. Commercially prepared paints in tubes vary greatly in quality. Versatile, they may be used opaquely, as glazes, or underpaintings, with or without dilution, thinly or thickly. A wide range of colors are available.

Palette: Surface for laying out and mixing paints, traditionally made from wood, though any non-absorbant surface is suitable. Ranging in size and design, most are held by a thumb hole. For acrylics, disposable paper and plastic palettes can be used. Watercolor, gouache, and tempera are generally mixed in china or plastic mixing trays with separate wells for color.

Palette knife: An implement used for mixing paint, applying thick impasto—a thickly applied paint that stands above the surface—and to scrape areas of wet oil paint to make corrections or for texture. The best are made with a forged blade diminishing in thickness for flexibility.

Pantone: The Pantone Matching System (PMS) is a system of corresponding color shades for a number of products and a variety of media. For example, colored papers, inks, and overlays will exactly match specifications for printing, if the PMS number is used to designate the color.

Paper: A sheet made of vegetable fibers matted together. Used as a support for watercolor, tempera, gouache, acrylics, pastels and drawings there are a myriad of varieties.
  Acid-free papers: Chemically neutral for long-lasting quality.
  Watercolor: Machine made with two deckle edges of consistent quality, but may lack strength and character of hand made.
  Rag watercolor papers sized with gelatine are highest quality.
  Weights: Expressed in pounds or grams per square meter. Lightest are 90 lbs. (190 gsm), heaviest 300 lbs. (610 gsm). Their surfaces can be hot pressed with a smooth surface with hardly any texture—which suits detailed styles of painting and flat, even applications of color— or cold pressed with a light, random grain suited to most methods of painting. Tooth, fine or smooth, describes the surface texture of board or paper.

Pastels: Pigment converted into stick form held by weak binding medium possessing a crumbly, powdery texture. Chalks are generally harder, as are crayons which are often smaller and more intensely colored. Commercial pastels may have as many as 500 shades and tints. Fixatives are used to stabilize the pastel painting surface.

Pencils: Graphite and clay bonded into a casing of cedar wood. Available in 20 degrees of hardness ranging from 9H (hardness) to 9B (blackness). HB is the middle range. Lead thickness ranges up to 1/8 inch. Best sharpened with utility knife or razor blade and repointed on fine sandpaper.

Percentage wheel or Proportion disk: A measuring device used to determine the percentages of enlargement or reduction of picture formats, similar in principle to a slide rule.

Plasticine: Commercial, oil-based modeling clay from which molds can be made.

Printmaking: A process by which an image is transferred from one surface, such as a plate or woodblock or stone, to paper (in general, though other material can be printed upon such as acetate or fabric). Some of the forms include:
  Intaglio (cutting below the surface) as in etching, engraving, aquatint, mezzotint.
  Relief (uneven surface) as in woodcut, linocut, photoengraving.
  Planograph (on the surface), as in lithograph, monotype.
  Stencil, as in silkscreen.

Projection: Optical devices to project photographic images for tracing or reference.
  Slide projectors: For 35mm slides
  Beloptican: Trade name of opaque projector for non-reflective images.

Rapidograph: The trade name for a fountain pen with a variety of nib sizes used primarily for technical drawing, but which can be used when an even line is required.

Respirator: A screen-like, filtered device worn over the mouth and nose to protect the respiratory system, used when airbrushing, or when using fixatives in unventilated areas.

Rubber cement pick-up: A rectangle of raw rubber used for swift removal and pick-up of excess dry cement.

Rub-down transfer: Sheets with adhesive backs are available in many patterns such as lines, dots, screen progressions, and letters in various typefaces which can be transferred by rubbing. Custom-made transfers can be produced by professionals or by using commercial systems available for studio use.

Scumbling: The action of dragging paint over a support, half covering it and leaving uneven, broken traces of color so the underlying paint or ground shows through.

Spray adhesive: Commercially prepared adhesives in aerosol cans for mounting artwork, type, acetate, paper and board.

Stenciling: Applying pigment through shapes cut from an impervious sheet held flush against the painting. High quality papers or heavy gauge tracing papers are acceptable, or thin plastic sheets (see Template).

Stipple: The application of a series of dots by dabbing with a brush at a right angle to the painting surface.

Support: The object upon which an image is created. There are many types beyond canvas, paper and all their varieties. Durability varies as well and must be considered when choosing supports.

Template: A guide used to render a precise shape. Standardized templates are generally made of plastic, but can be custom-made from heavy paper or vellum or cardboard.

Thinner: Materials used to thin paints for a specific consistency or for workability. Theoretically, they have a temporary effect and should evaporate during drying. They are often solvents as well. Turpentine, less expensive mineral spirits, and alcohol (which is often used for clean up), and water, are most common forms.

Transparent dyes: Available in jars and bottles, dyes stain and permeate paper and become waterproof when dry. Their brilliant colors can be utilized at full strength or in thin washes.

Underpainting: The first application of paint when utilizing a layered technique. Made in flat broad strokes, it assumes a later stage in the layering process when it will visually combine with subsequent layers to create specific effects.

Varnish: A hard, glossy oil-based substance used to coat a surface with a transparent protective layer. Paint clarity may be improved by its application as well as increased durability of the finish.

Vellum: Technically, a paper-like material made from calf-skin used as a water-based media support. The name applies to smooth, high-quality papers which resemble the real material.

Wacom tablet: Used in computer illustration, a surface upon which to draw with a stylus, which electronically transfers the line to a computer screen.

Washes: A thin, exceptionally fluid application of color made by excessively diluting paint with an appropriate thinner. Unlike glazes, no additional medium is present. Opaque colors can be applied as a wash.

Watercolor: Finely ground pigment suspended in gum arabic—a water-soluble binder. Available in tubes and pans. Fast-drying and quick to use, pure watercolor painting is based on the use of transparent washes with highlights being rendered by the white paper beneath. Generally used on paper, can be combined with other media.

Wet in wet: The action of painting into a color layer that is still wet so that the newly applied color can be worked with the existing paint.

Wet over dry: The action of painting onto a dry paint layer, so that the newly applied color does not disturb the underlying layers.

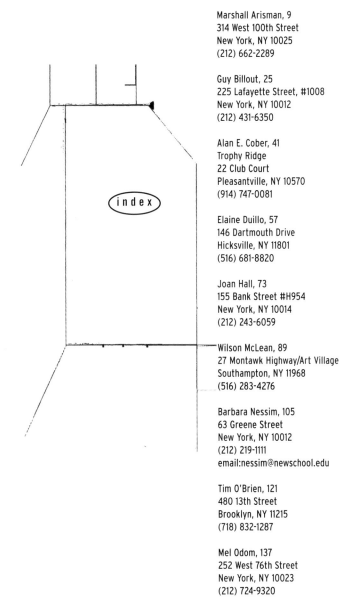

Gratitude goes to President Vincent DiFate and the Board of Directors of the Society of Illustrators for their support. Special thanks to Honorary President Howard Munce and Graphic Artists Guild Director Paul Basista for their fine words, and especially to Society of Illustrators Director, Terrence Brown, for his support throughout. Bravos to spouse/photographers Rosemary Howard and John Duillo and to Marianne Barcelona for her sensitivity to the artists' work. Delight with Stephen Byram and Eric Baker's exciting design. Thanks to copy editor Arpi Ermoyan for her endless care. Most grateful thanks to Brian Morris at Rotovision for his unwavering belief in the project, and to Angie Patchell for her cheerful help. Deepest thanks to Publications Chairman, Jerry McConnell, for his generous guidance. And, of course, appreciation beyond measure to the nine talented illustrators who shared their gifts so readily and with such good grace.